M000107806

# FURNITURE
## IN THE
# *Southern Style*

# FURNITURE IN THE
## *Southern Style*

## 27 SHOP DRAWINGS OF FURNITURE
### FROM THE
## MUSEUM OF EARLY SOUTHERN
## DECORATIVE ARTS

### WITH A FOREWORD BY MACK S. HEADLEY, JR.
# ROBERT W. LANG & GLEN D. HUEY

POPULAR WOODWORKING BOOKS
CINCINNATI, OHIO

# Table of Contents

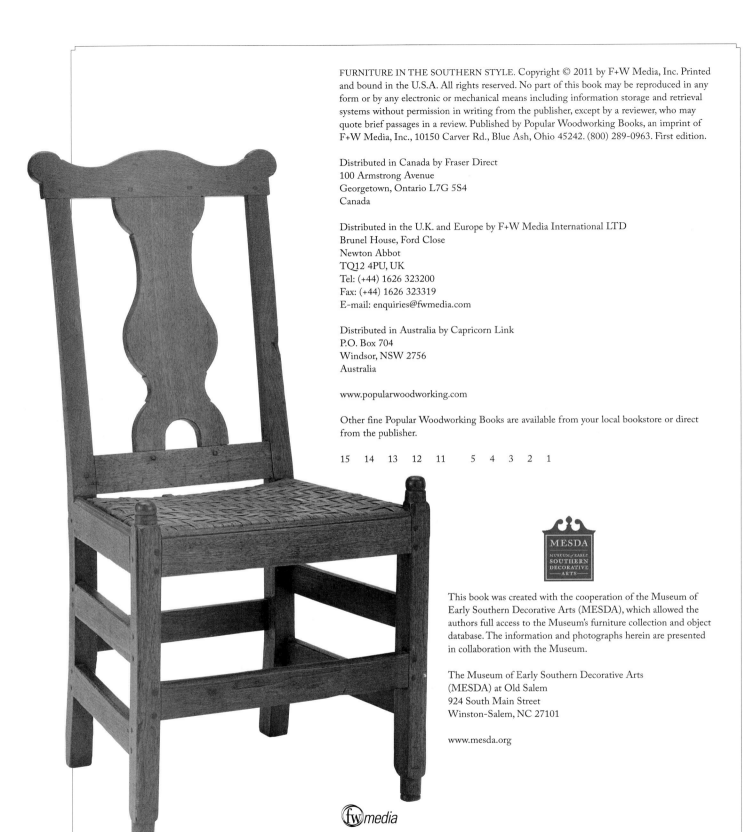

FURNITURE IN THE SOUTHERN STYLE. Copyright © 2011 by F+W Media, Inc. Printed and bound in the U.S.A. All rights reserved. No part of this book may be reproduced in any form or by any electronic or mechanical means including information storage and retrieval systems without permission in writing from the publisher, except by a reviewer, who may quote brief passages in a review. Published by Popular Woodworking Books, an imprint of F+W Media, Inc., 10150 Carver Rd., Blue Ash, Ohio 45242. (800) 289-0963. First edition.

Distributed in Canada by Fraser Direct
100 Armstrong Avenue
Georgetown, Ontario L7G 5S4
Canada

Distributed in the U.K. and Europe by F+W Media International LTD
Brunel House, Ford Close
Newton Abbot
TQ12 4PU, UK
Tel: (+44) 1626 323200
Fax: (+44) 1626 323319
E-mail: enquiries@fwmedia.com

Distributed in Australia by Capricorn Link
P.O. Box 704
Windsor, NSW 2756
Australia

www.popularwoodworking.com

Other fine Popular Woodworking Books are available from your local bookstore or direct from the publisher.

15    14    13    12    11        5    4    3    2    1

This book was created with the cooperation of the Museum of Early Southern Decorative Arts (MESDA), which allowed the authors full access to the Museum's furniture collection and object database. The information and photographs herein are presented in collaboration with the Museum.

The Museum of Early Southern Decorative Arts (MESDA) at Old Salem
924 South Main Street
Winston-Salem, NC 27101

www.mesda.org

fw media

*Publisher:* Steve Shanesy
*Copy Editor:* Megan Fitzpatrick
*Production Coordinator:* Mark Griffin
*Design & Layout:* Linda Watts
*Photos:* Courtesy of the Museum of Early Southern Decorative Arts
*Illustrations:* Robert W. Lang & Glen D. Huey

# Foreword

∞

I haven't studied the pieces chosen for this publication individually nor do I know the biographies of the individual makers; some probably exist. I only know this furniture through these drawings and photographs, like you, if you have looked into the book. Why am I qualified to introduce these pieces? Well, I have made a lot of furniture and much of it was done by copying the style of 18th-century craftsmen, with the construction accomplished with hand tools.

I have confidence about the integrity of 18th-century work, in general, because the pieces represent work that has been tested and has endured. There are special things about these pieces. Some of this furniture survives because it has had unusual loving care, but all of the pieces are strong. The drawings of these pieces show familiar construction and art.

## Access to Original Objects

Museums differ greatly in how fully they are able to share their intellectual property. Some allow access for personal patterns but worry about commercial exploitation. Part of my museum cabinetmaking job (at the Anthony Hay Cabinet Shop in Colonial Williamsburg) is to share 18th-century cabinetmaking processes and design principles. Dimensioned drawings are discouraged. Another situation where specifics might be withheld is when you have access to other institution's pieces. Then the institution, as a courtesy, protects the partner institution's property and lets their partner make their own decisions about their collections. Licensing fees for access to their collections provides some income for museums. This income can be an important resource for cash-starved non-profit foundations.

These worries don't burden this book. The research-driven philosophy the Museum of Early Southern Decorative Arts (MESDA) has taken here addresses a need for accurate construction, scale and detail from original furniture. The information contained in these drawings will be of great value to traditional woodworking. This group of drawings shares Southern building culture in the best tradition of an educational foundation. I hope other institutions from other regions will see this kind of publication as a valuable part of their educational mission. It will be good if the MESDA and *Popular Woodworking Magazine* cooperation proves a success.

Making any of these pieces that are owned by MESDA would be an excellent excuse to visit the museum (located in Winston-Salem, N.C.) and see the work you want to reproduce. Seeing the physical object and the rest of the museum's inspiring collection would be a rewarding experience for any practicing or aspiring woodworker. Finding an errant tool mark, layout line or compass center left by the maker enhances the humanity in a piece and gives insights into process and your path to produce the object.

## Who Made these Pieces?

There is a lot to like about this group of drawings. By nature decoration is self-conscious, but there is an honesty and practicality in these pieces that is very unselfconscious and endearing. These pieces are a study group from MESDA's great museum collection and object database. The theme is "furniture from people who earned their living making things," but not just any furniture, principally joiner's furniture.

Outside of urban centers joiners were the best woodworkers; their skills were honed decorating architectural interiors. Large numbers of immigrants brought European woodworking to the backcountry but I would guess that many of the makers of these pieces seldom traveled more than 20 miles from their home base. Their markets overlapped with other enclaves of workmen whose works reflect tradition and the integration of new ideas filtering through a design network that extended across the landscape south and concentrated around settled communities.

Traveling 20 miles in a wagon or on a horse to build a house or barn was, most likely, not uncommon. Craftsmen were dispersed through the settled areas; they came together on big projects and found other ways to keep busy between architectural projects. Some worked for bosses, others worked independently.

From their architectural work, craftsmen brought to making furniture their understanding of geometry, wood selection, tool preference and tool maintenance for the processing of materials, cutting joints and decoration.

### Available Drawings

Drawings of architectural designs available to 18th-century craftsmen imparted rules for the size of structural posts, horizontal beams and the scaling of molding profiles. The drawings could be used as reference for trimming roof cornices, door frames, making doors, windows and stairways.

In England, published rules and drawings in Sebastiano Serlio's "Five Books of Architecture" circulated from 1611. It is believed to be the first illustrated book of architectural design printed in Europe. Serlio's book is illustrated with woodcuts and instruction for craftsmen's geometry, drawing in perspective, examples of ancient Roman structures, and Serlio's renaissance Italian architectural reproductions with bold moldings sheltering lower structure and highlighting foundations. Serlio's molding profiles are especially satisfying.

Brothers Thomas and Batty Langley were prolific publishers of architectural designs. Historians suggest their drawings were motivated by a Masonic mission to advance the building trades. Their 1756 "The City and Country Builder's and Workman's Treasury of Design" touched on furniture with some informative fractional layouts of some casework and pier tables, but their designs are too lofty for the general market.

I am in awe of the designs in Thomas Chippendale's 1754, 1755 and 1762 editions of the "Gentleman and Cabinet-Maker's Director," but as a source of patterns, most of Chippendale's drawings have a complexity

problem and to execute them a team of specialists would be needed. Chippendale had a good market with many customers drilled in calligraphy's nuance of curve, who expected finesse and novelty in their furniture.

There are a couple of modern measured drawing collections I especially like, including Wallace Nutting's third volume of his "Furniture Treasury" and Gustav Ecke's "Chinese Domestic Furniture." I like Nutting for the quality of curve. Ecke for that, too, but also for his illustration of structure.

The drawings in this book of pieces from MESDA's collection and object database satisfy my eye in capturing the kind of structure, art and honesty I have seen in 18th-century furniture. The isometric drawings are an especially good representation of the specifics and complexity of the structures. *Popular Woodworking Magazine* should be proud of its work.

### Taking Advantage of These Designs

As a study group, these drawings offer numerous alternative structures, patterns for turning, inlay, molding profiles and scalloped work. Studying these designs with a belief that each maker had a plan that you can see reflected through their pieces' measurements makes the designs more valuable than just as references for individual building projects.

What, for example, did these makers think was good foundation for different pieces? The variety of bracket feet in this collection gives 10 structural, proportional and decorative options. There are six cornice moldings and many more moldings used to finish the top trimming of pieces. Nearly every piece involves the use of a compass to lay out moldings, scallops and inlay patterns.

I have tried using the Pinwheel Cabinet (on page 144) as a proportional study and was gratified to find that it is a square dressed up with layers of intermediate and finer-scale detail reflected through decisions about the stock dimensions, moldings and inlay. The pinwheel inlay appears to be a third of the basic chosen square, and the feet are a seventh of the height up to the top of the horizontal molding that flanks the arched top. These are architectural ratios found in Serlio's books.

There are also antique furniture collectors and dealers who thrive on the kind of information this book captures. Recognizing the design and evidence of hand-tool technology, which distinguishes preindustrial production, is one of the collector's most important assets.

## How Good is This Construction?

Are we seeing the best 18th-century construction? The craftsmen who made these pieces did special things with their experience. Their work is in a museum. Look for places you think novelty conflicts with economy or structure. There are eccentricities in these pieces that the makers chose in trying to distinguish their work for their local customers. There is a lot of practical economy in this study group and some pure novelty. Can you improve a piece? What is your Platonic ideal?

I know you are going to play with these designs. Do you have to adapt execution to your tools? Fine. You can change it, but have you improved it? Use what you learn from these pieces when you want to design your own work. I have learned the most when I looked for the tool choice, layout control and most efficient wood-removal technique available to the first builder. How can you learn from a good example if you are already doing something else? I have tried teaching inquisitiveness, and I hope for a lot of it from my students.

There are 27 examples here. Do all of these pieces illustrate a different person's plan? How did one shop or one man decide how to do things? There are groups of pieces extant that show how a specific shop expressed itself in casework, table and chair work. Those bodies of work would make a good theme for a drawing book.

The men who made these things also expected to maintain them. Reversibility is designed in knowing how to soften the hide glue, and knowing the direct proper force for disassembly was considered a part of good construction.

The construction is good when it gets your project done and you have developed some new skills or bought some new tools.

## How Accurately Can These Pieces Be Reproduced?

There are a lot of dovetails. The one area I think could be improved in the drawings is the dovetail representation. They look mechanical. Every piece of wood in the pieces selected for drawing was hand-planed and all the dovetails were cut by hand. Hand production was part of the original maker's daily work and it will be hard to avoid some of it in making any of these pieces.

For example, how much molding work will you do with a plane, a router, gouges, scrapers, or maybe a table saw to set fillets? Be careful with the table saw and plan a strategy to have solid support for the piece you are cutting. Handwork has an aesthetic quality under finish, unlike the lack of surface dimension of machined work.

Take advantage of your jointer, planer, table saw, band saw, mortising machine and dovetail jig to make these pieces. Go for it and be careful. Please don't compromise the structure to accommodate your machines and don't compromise the quality of curve captured in the drawings. Most important are the moldings. Profiles of moldings are your best opportunity to work with the light on your surface. I'll stop preaching. You just go out and make something and learn from it.

I love drawing and design. I am looking forward to more of this.

MACK S. HEADLEY, JR.
Master Cabinetmaker, Anthony Hay Cabinet Shop
at Colonial Williamsburg

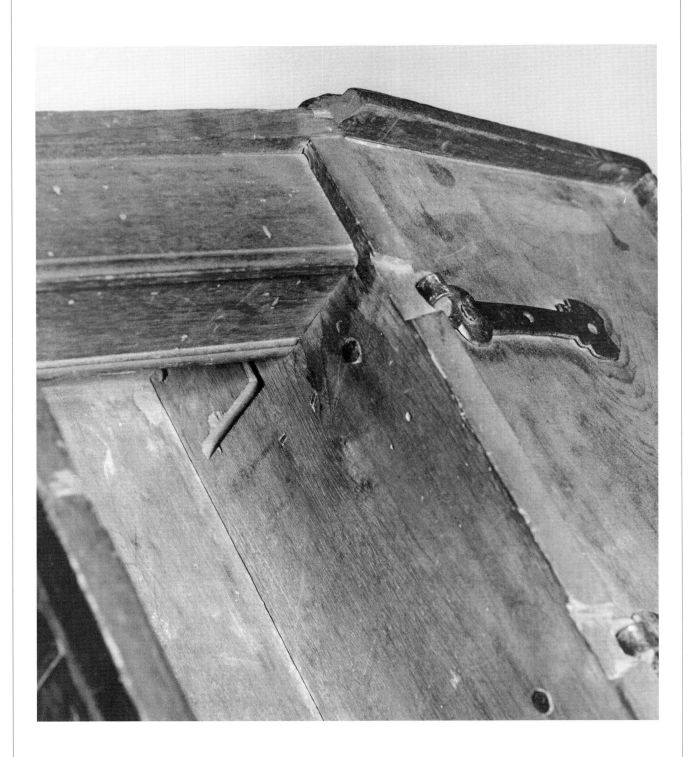

# Overview

# *Introduction*

⌒

Our understanding of the past is based on brief glimpses of small portions of a picture rather than a broad panorama, and for every fact we know for certain, there are hundreds that leave us guessing. Most of what we know comes from observing physical objects, or from reading what someone chose to write. It's easy to think that the topics written about were the most important or most predominant in the period. That isn't always or even often the case.

Beyond objects, the best source to understand the past comes from those who did the work during the time in question. Those sources are rare. Our cabinetmaking ancestors didn't leave detailed descriptions of what they did; they left their work and a few subtle clues in the form of invoices and estate records.

To understand period furniture and how it was made, we rely on someone who looks back in time and tries to explain what was done from a different point of view, in different circumstances and often without practical experience in building furniture. History isn't so much about facts as it is about guesses based on varying degrees of education and prejudice.

Cultural shifts and events that don't appear connected affect our knowledge of the past. This book is about furniture made in the southern United States between 1650 and 1830. But the Civil War, which was 30 years after that period, has a lot to do with our knowledge and perceptions of Southern furniture. History is written by the winners, and in the case of published material about American furniture, one might assume that outside the area between Philadelphia and Boston, few if any Americans in the 18th century had more than the crudest chairs, tables, beds or cases in their homes.

For every book or museum exhibition about Southern furniture there have been a dozen or more about Northeastern (primarily New England) furniture. The general cultural impression held in the northern United States is that in the years prior to the American Revolution, the American South was a rural, backward and sparsely populated place.

### The Civilized South of the 1700s

In reality, the South was a more settled, civilized, diverse and safer region than the North throughout the 18th century and well into the 19th century. Almost every town had its resident cabinetmaker, towns weren't very far apart and they existed as part of a larger and cohesive society.

The standard view of American history consists of the settling of Jamestown in Virginia, the arrival of the pilgrims in Massachusetts and a bit of fighting with the Native population. Then we fast forward 150 years to the American Revolution. The period when the furniture in this book was made is mostly skipped altogether, or at best glossed over.

Boston, New York and Philadelphia are depicted in our history books as major metropolitan areas, while Baltimore, Norfolk and Charleston are barely mentioned. At the time, Charleston was larger and wealthier than Philadelphia and far more cosmopolitan. The well-to-do in Charleston often imported furniture directly from England, while Philadelphians tended to purchase locally.

The furniture of Charleston has been well documented in "The Furniture of Charleston: 1680-1820" by Bradford L. Rauschenberg and John Bivins, Jr., and by Samuel A. Humphrey in "Thomas Elfe

Cabinetmaker." This formal, high-style furniture was every bit the equal, and often better than, similar pieces from the Northeast. There was a closer connection in the cabinetmaking trade in Charleston to what was current in England than there was in Philadelphia, New York or Boston.

## Typical Furniture for a Typical Home

In this book we examine other pieces, furniture that was not formal and not urban. This type of furniture is abundant in the MESDA collection and object database, but not often seen in other places. We hope this book serves as an introduction to typical pieces of the place and period and gives a broader view of how furniture was made in the early years of what is now the United States. The typical piece of 18th-century furniture was not the mahogany highboy of which you might think. This is true of both the South and the North. That highboy comes to mind because that is what we see when we go to museums or when we browse book covers. It's natural for a museum to feature the best and most expensive pieces it can find, but it's foolish to think that is a representation of the period as a whole. Then as now, such pieces weren't seen very often in typical homes.

If we want to understand the furniture of a particular time, we need to look through a wider lens and consider where the people who made the furniture lived, how they got there, and how they learned and practiced their trade. If we focus on a narrow area, we'll likely miss most of what we're looking for.

Northeastern cultural bias led to the founding of the Museum of Early Southern Decorative Arts (MESDA) in the 1960s. The spark was a comment by Joseph Downs, curator of the American Wing of the Metropolitan Museum of Art, who stated that little of significance was ever made south of Baltimore. The Southern response was to ask if the statement was made "out of prejudice or out of ignorance." It was followed by the efforts of Frank L. Horton and his mother, Theodosia Taliaferro, in the study, collection and documentation of Southern arts.

MESDA is different than most museums. It was built on a foundation of regional pride, filled with thousands of examples and staffed with people dedicated to sharing the collection and their knowledge. The MESDA collection and research databases are available for anyone to study, and in the near future that material will be accessible online. When the database is online, you'll be able to examine the photographs and documents that we studied as we researched and worked on the drawings in this book.

Chances are you'll feel as we did; that is, overwhelmed with the quality and diversity of early Southern furniture. We also hope you'll be inspired to travel to Winston-Salem, N.C., where you can see in person many of the pieces in this book, both at the museum and in the adjacent village of Old Salem.

Our original thinking was that this book would present a comprehensive look at Southern furniture produced outside the major cities, in a less-than-formal style. Like Downs, we first had to get over our Yankee ignorance and arrogance and look at what was in front of us. The abundance and diversity of pieces in the MESDA collection and object database left us to offer but a small taste of an incredible feast.

Limited by the available space in this book, we chose pieces we felt were representative in two ways. We looked for common forms, then for good examples and interesting variations of those forms. As furniture makers we are intrigued by the unusual, and fascinated by pieces that survive even if they break the "rules" of design and construction. We looked for pieces that appealed to us personally, things we would reproduce and place in our homes. It wasn't a scientific or scholarly approach, but this is a book written for and by furniture makers, not scholars.

The difficult part was deciding which pieces had to be left out. Our initial selections would have produced a book three or four times the size of this one, and as we worked it became harder to let pieces go. Other authors would have made different selections to arrive at a collection of pieces equal to this.

We also left out pieces that have been covered elsewhere, even though they fit our criteria. We didn't include the work of Thomas Day, so we suggest you read "Thomas Day – African American Furniture Maker" by Rodney D. Barfield and Patricia P. Marshall. There are several other excellent books about specific makers and regions, many of them available at the MESDA bookstore.

This book is not by any means the final word on "not formal, not urban" early Southern furniture. It is a study of contrasts between different regions of the early American South, between past and current times, and the differences between what we've been taught and what we have left to learn.

— *Robert W. Lang & Glen D. Huey*

# About the Furniture

The builders of the furniture pieces in this book were a diverse group, separated from us and each other by geography and time. For most we know nothing beyond the work they left behind. For others we know only similar pieces that survived the years. For a few, we have a name and perhaps a trace of their lives from period documents. We don't know much about the people; we only know the furniture that survived longer than the recollection of their lives and names.

We can't make blanket statements about them, but there are trends and tendencies that help explain how the furniture was made, and why details in these pieces differ from what we might expect. These builders were an important cross section of a long-lived craft tradition and the culture of their times

The pieces in this book were built between the early 1700s and the early 1800s, and most were made by professional makers working in small towns. Some may have specialized in furniture making, but most were more general woodworkers. Urban areas were able to support distinct groups such as joiners, cabinetmakers and turners, but the work we see in this book was made by men who combined these skills and specialties.

As the inland areas of the South became settled, small towns developed at more or less regular intervals. For a given amount of farmland, a community equipped to support the agricultural enterprises developed. These small towns would have a church, and several tradesmen, such as weavers, potters, blacksmiths, gunsmiths and woodworkers. A small-town woodworker would build doors, windows and trim for houses, caskets for the dead, and crates for shipping in addition to furniture.

In southern coastal cities, cabinetmakers had a closer connection to styles and techniques that were current in England than did cabinetmakers living in the North. The northern cities had definitive styles because early immigrants established themselves in trades and stayed put. In the South, immigration of skilled tradesmen continued much longer as the western regions became settled, and most of the growth in the South was from internal sources, a growing population and migration from other colonies.

Much of the North remained unsettled wilderness until well after the American Revolution. Even today, much of New York, Pennsylvania and Massachusetts are more sparsely settled than the inland areas of Virginia and the Carolinas.

A cabinetmaker who trained in England or another European country and then came to America had options in the 1700s, unless he came as an indentured servant. In the South there were more opportunities for immigrants, both in the port cities and in new and growing settlements farther inland. In the North growth didn't continue due west, it went west until faced with mountains or hostile Native Americans about 150 miles from the coast, then headed south. The settled areas in the North consisted of ethnic or religious groups that were well established, and not always open to newcomers. Many Europeans who landed in the Northeast eventually moved on and settled in the South.

In colonial Virginia and North Carolina, settlements were established hundreds of miles farther inland than in the North, they were closer together, and were often a mix of residents whose roots were from different areas of Europe. The growth of the

American South was largely fed by immigrants from other colonies who were in search of land and a more congenial climate. Settlement in the western portions was encouraged early on. As the inland population grew, towns tended to reach an optimal size, then neighboring towns were established close by.

Skilled tradesmen of the day were respected members of the community, and had acquired their skills in apprenticeships with established artisans. In large cities in England and Europe, the apprentice system was well established and in the larger cities of the American colonies the system was similar. When a boy reached the age of 12 or 13, his father would arrange with a master to take the boy on to learn a trade. In return for training, the master would gain a skilled employee. In the course of his education the boy would receive little or no wages, but would be housed, fed and often provided with basic tools.

Apprentices earned their keep by doing basic tasks, and it was in the master's interest to develop an apprentice's skills as quickly as possible. A fast learner could become a journeyman in a few years. In the early years of colonization, tradesmen brought their skills with them. It was a scenario of opportunity; in a developing area, a journeyman could become a master in less time than it would take in the old country.

In the growing colonies, communities and the businesses within them tended to grow to optimal sizes and then operate at that level. The concepts of "bigger is always better" and "growth is always good" were in the future. A typical urban cabinetmaker's shop would consist of a master, several journeymen and a few apprentices. In small towns, a shop might be half the size of an urban shop, and in little villages the local cabinetmaker might well be one man and his sons. These local enterprises operated under similar traditions; a skilled artisan knew his trade by what he had been taught, and he would pass those same skills and methods on to those he trained.

## Breaking the Mold

In large urban communities, both in the colonies and in Europe, tradition played a significant role in how furniture was made. Competition existed among shops, so deviation from standard methods would be seen as inferior work. In the rural areas of the colonies, however, the local cabinetmaker was the only option, and if he decided he didn't much care for certain methods, he was free to follow his own prefer-

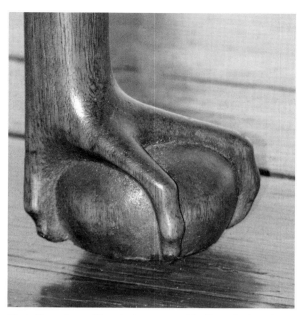

*Details such as this mis-interpreted ball-and-claw foot were the exception rather than the rule. Most Southern furniture was more in keeping with current styles.*

ences. If he trained an apprentice, he could teach his way, not necessarily the methods he had been taught.

As journeymen cabinetmakers headed west or south in search of opportunities, they took along the methods they'd learned; we see that migration of methods in many of the details on the pieces in this book. Basic forms are similar to those made in large cities or on the Continent, but there are variations in details such as feet, moldings and joinery. These American cabinetmakers were loosely connected to their more urban contemporaries; small towns were not isolated, but travel wasn't easy. We found old advertisements for mail-order hardware, and it is likely that a resident of a small inland town would make an annual or semi-annual trip to the closest coastal town. This distant and tenuous connection meant freedom of expression for a rural cabinetmaker. A customer would have to travel far to compare his work to another's, and there wouldn't be local competitors to speak of idiosyncrasies as defects.

This distant-but-not-too-far relationship between cabinetmakers in small towns and work in larger communities led to some of the more interesting pieces in the MESDA collection and object database. Some of these pieces seem to have been built from a description, as if a client saw a piece in Charleston, then at a later date went to his local cabinetmaker to have something similar made. The client's memory and communication skills, combined with the cabinetmaker's never having seen the real thing, led to pieces where common elements are present, but executed in unusual ways.

Most of the furniture in this book was made for clients of means but not great wealth. A modern reproduction of a large Philadelphia case piece takes a lot of time to produce, and would bear a significantly high price. The same would be true of an original piece worked to that level of style and detail; not everyone could afford such an expensive status symbol. Then as now, time is money when it comes to building furniture. What is common in most museum collections is not what was common during the period.

### Hidden Strength

Variations and cost considerations aside, the pieces in this book were made well enough to have survived intact for a long time. The primary means of joinery was the dovetail for case and box assemblies, and the mortise-and-tenon (often pinned or drawbored) for tables and frame-and-panel assemblies. Variations among forms of dovetails are found throughout the pieces in this book, and attitudes about this joint are different among woodworkers today than they were in the period this book covers.

Today, we see dovetails as a testament to the maker's skill. We want our dovetails to be perfect, and expect to see them front and center. When these pieces were built, the dovetail was viewed in a different light, valued for its strength and durability over appearance.

In many instances, dovetails joining case sides to tops and bottoms were covered with molding, or fabricated so that the joint was hidden. In the Lady's Desk on page 132, dovetails join the top of the upper case to the sides, but the joint is hidden from both directions. The maker used dovetails for strength, but took extra steps to ensure that the only visible part of the joint was a narrow band of end grain showing on the side.

Where dovetails are visible, they are neat in appearance but far from perfect. This is also the case with drawer dovetails. Lipped to be half-blind from the outside of the case, drawer dovetails on most pieces were good enough to endure, but it is obvious from their appearance that the builders were moving at a productive pace, unaware that in a future time they would be subjected to the scrutiny of makers with different values. If the drawer was strong and fit neatly in its opening, no one stayed awake at night wondering if a better marking knife or more expensive saw would make their dovetails look better.

Another common detail that stands out to the modern eye is the use of nails and wooden pegs as fasteners. In the blanket chest on page 128, the feet are nailed to the base molding that is nailed to the case bottom. That, in turn, is nailed to the dovetailed box.

*Wooden pegs were often used as visible fasteners, as were nails which were often used to attach moldings.*

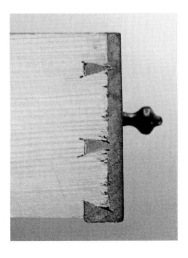

*Dovetails were intended to hold parts together; they were not showy details as they are often considered today (especially if out of sight in a drawer).*

The Stretcher Table on page 24 has the top attached to the stretchers with wooden pegs driven in from above. Modern workers will go to great lengths to avoid showing nail holes, but nailing from the outside was an accepted and common practice in the day.

Nails were also used to attach drawer runners and drawer guides to the insides of cases and tables. Simple guides to support the drawers were far more common than complex internal frames. For many pieces we don't show how a top attaches to a frame below; your guess would be as valid as ours. Common methods at the time would be to provide a cleat on the inside and attach a top with screws from below, or use pocket screws. If those methods make you nervous about wood movement, cabinetmaker's buttons in slots or figure-8 connectors would also work.

One of the details that will likely cause distress to some readers is the fact that on many pieces, drawer bottoms and case bottoms are attached with nails only. There are many possible explanations for this, the most logical of which is the reduction in time nailing provides. In the period, nails weren't cheap, but they were readily available, and the savings in time from not having to run a series of grooves with a plow plane would offset the cost of the fasteners.

As much as our modern sensibilities may howl over the practice, the MESDA database is full of pieces with intact nailed-on drawer and case bottoms. They have survived quite nicely for a couple hundred years. At the other extreme, some of the more refined pieces have drawer bottoms held in with slips, a common method in high-quality English furniture.

## Materials

Most of the component lumber is thicker and wider than what is common today. While some of this material may have been riven or sawn by the cabinetmaker, it's more likely that the raw lumber came from a local or nearby sawmill. Not every town could support a mill with its own needs, but a mill could get along nicely serving several towns within a day's wagon ride. Sawmills are an early sign that an area being settled is becoming civilized, filling the needs for building construction and farm implements with lesser lumber along with the better-quality stuff destined to be made into furniture.

The most common primary material found in these pieces is walnut, with poplar or pine as a secondary wood. This reflects the abundance of resources in the area, which was likely appreciated by cabinetmakers arriving from England or Europe where wood had been logged and milled for centuries and quality material was scarce. Wide, clear pieces are seen in tabletops, sides of chests and cabinets and backs of case pieces. When you can make a back from four planks for a cabinet that is 7' tall and 5' wide, you're obviously in an area where wood is abundant.

*Bottoms of carcases and drawers were often nailed from below. In this blanket chest, nails hold the feet to the molding, and the molding to the box.*

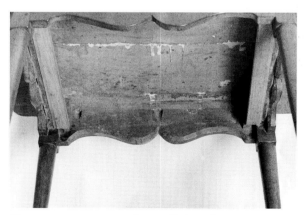

*Drawer runners were often nailed, and tops were attached with pocket screws. The pockets could be made with a brace and bit, or a few cuts with a chisel or gouge.*

Walnut is an excellent wood for furniture, and American walnut was favored in English furniture of the period. The choice of wood is a balance between the appearance and durability of the finished piece and the ease in working with it. Walnut ranks high in both areas. The wood appeals visually, and the grain structure is such that the material is hard enough to hold fine details, but not so hard as to be difficult or unpredictable to work.

The builders of the pieces in this book had the advantage of being among the first to make commercial use of the abundant resources of the area. One of the major assets of the American colonies to the British (as well as to the colonists) was the availability and variety of timber. American hardwoods were used in English furniture, and the Royal Navy needed long, straight trunks of New England pine for masts, and knees from southern live oaks for curved supports inside hulls.

Colonists needed houses, barns and stores, merchants needed wagons, buckets and barrels, and everyone needed chairs, tables and containers for their possessions. In areas where land was being converted to agricultural use, trees were often more of a liability than an asset. Land was cleared to grow tobacco, a crop that quickly depleted the soil, and more areas were cleared of trees in a few year's time.

## Background & Influences

The quick and easy version of Southern history is that the area was settled by the English, who established large plantations for the production of cotton and tobacco. That is indeed part of the story, but there were other groups of immigrants whose origins were in other parts of Europe, or from other American colonies. These groups brought with them different cultures, and those cultures included different forms of agriculture, and different styles and methods for producing furniture.

The growth and development of the South was more internal than external. Much of the South was settled by groups moving from other areas of America, not directly from Europe. In many cases a generation or two separated a family's arrival in America and its arrival in North Carolina or Virginia.

The ruling classes in Virginia were rich in land, and their methods of planting, using up the soil then moving on, pushed them west from the coast. Settlement of the western areas was encouraged in part

to provide a buffer between settled areas and Native Americans, and in part to remove groups such as the Scots away from the English population. The Scots weren't fond of the English either, and were happy to establish themselves in their own distant areas.

There were also large groups of Germans and other Eastern Europeans. The Moravian community at Salem was significant both for the size of the settle-

*Being first to use the abundant resources of southern woodlands meant the availability of clear, wide material.*

ment and the fact that much of the infrastructure and furnishings of Salem stayed in place. The Moravians also were thorough record keepers so there is a good deal of information available at Old Salem Museums & Gardens, of which MESDA is an important component.

Johannes Krause was the master cabinetmaker in Salem in the last quarter of the 18th century and the builder of the desk with bookcase on page 56. There are several similar desks in the community. Krause was trained in Europe, and Salem records mention several of his apprentices, and his displeasure with some of them. The Moravians were more closely connected with communities in Pennsylvania than with larger cities in the South. As might be expected, this work bears a closer resemblance to German and Pennsylvania forms than English work of the period.

Many of the other pieces in this book are closely related to English styles of the period, as might be expected. The closeness of that relation varies considerably from piece to piece. Some are nearly identical to English forms and others bear only traces of their ancestry. This is especially evident in bracket feet, a detail that is by nature troublesome.

Within this book are formal bracket feet that are shaped across the width and molded along the edge, as well as simple, flat bracket feet with a curved lower edge as the only decorative element. You'll see several methods to attach the corners of the feet to each other and to the case. There are bracket feet that appear too tall, too squat, too stout and too delicate. All of these are reflections of the original makers and their approaches to solving problems and resolving details.

As we made these drawings, we tried to connect with the men behind the work. Their personalities come through as you study the pieces, especially if you question what it is you see. These were talented builders, but they had their quirks and idiosyncrasies as all humans do. Their lack of perfection proves their humanity, and the details of the pieces teach us more about the makers, their times, their methods and their tools than any possible written description.

### About the Drawings

The drawings in this book were prepared from photographs of pieces in the MESDA object database, and many of the actual pieces are in the collections of MESDA and Old Salem Museums & Gardens. Most of the photos were taken by researchers and some were

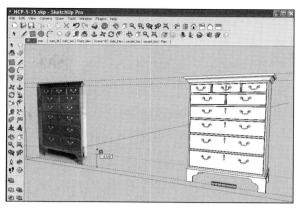

*Photos imported into SketchUp are scaled to their actual size; then parts of the object can be measured.*

taken by the authors. With most pieces we had several images from different points of view and a first-hand look at the furniture itself, but some drawings were made with only one or two available photographs. Measurements were derived from overall dimensions listed in the information sheets for each piece.

If we had an unlimited budget and unlimited time, we would have examined and measured each piece, then made a copy to be sure we were right. That wasn't an option, but we feel relatively confident that these drawings reflect an accurate description of the pieces. The degree of accuracy varies somewhat, and there are places where we had to make educated assumptions, especially for inner details.

As experienced furniture builders, we feel our assumptions are sound, and close enough for the purposes of building these pieces. We also believe that most readers will probably change some aspects as they build. Overall form and proportion are more important than arguments over the exact sizes of tenons or the thickness of drawer backs.

The drawings began as three-dimensional models, rendered in Google SketchUp. Scanned images were imported into the computer and scaled to known dimensions. Within the program, we were able to zoom in on the images and measure as we worked on the computer models. Obviously, this isn't the same as taking physical measurements of the actual pieces, but we're confident that we at worst came very close.

Our goal wasn't to enable our readers to make exact copies of these pieces, but to give a good sense of the proportions, details and methods of construction in the originals. We saw a variety of methods in construction, and if we were making reproductions of any of these pieces, we would introduce our own variations of technique. We would also feel free to use these drawings as a starting point, to adapt what we see to our own needs and techniques we might favor.

## Buckle Up Your 18th-century Shoes

As we worked, we regularly asked each other about one detail or another. Nearly every model evoked a discussion of methods, details and the choices made by the builder. Many of these pieces violate what today are considered as "rules" for building furniture.

Today's rules come from yesterday's book or magazine article, but the makers of these pieces followed rules handed down to them or methods that worked for them. Few woodworkers today would be able to nail on the bottom of a drawer or cabinet without feeling guilty, but many of these pieces show exactly that construction. It's hard to label a technique as "wrong" when you see an example that's been around for a couple of centuries.

We set some ground rules with the first few pieces we modeled. Within the limitations of working from photographs, we decided to be as accurate as we could be. Nearly every piece in this book is built from lumber that is thicker than standard sizes of today. We resisted the temptation to draw anything thinner than what we saw in order to make a reader's trip to the lumberyard easier or less expensive. If you're building one of these pieces, you can choose to make substitutions of this sort, but we didn't want to make those decisions for all of our readers.

We also decided to include all of the joinery in our models, even though those details aren't always seen in the finished drawings. This leads to a higher degree of accuracy in the models, and that in turn leads to better two-dimensional drawings that derive from the three-dimensional models. The models themselves are available in SketchUp format (see the back page of this book for information on ordering), and this gives readers the opportunity to take the models apart on their computers to examine the details. It also gives the reader who wants to modify or adapt one of these pieces a head start on creating a new model.

## Detective Work/Guesswork

When we came to a place where we weren't sure about a detail, we made our best guesses and used details we considered to be either best or typical

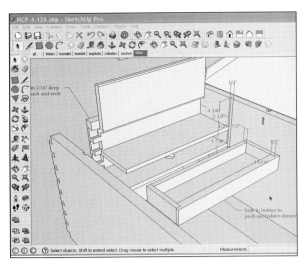

*In the model, details of joints and construction are added, as they would be in a real piece of furniture.*

practices of the period. In many cases, the builder's personality and work habits showed in more obvious places, and we made decisions about hidden details based on that. Many of our conversations over the course of this work revolved around this question: "If a guy used this method here, what would he likely do there?"

The drawings for each piece were generated by exporting two-dimensional views from the SketchUp models to our page layout software. Dimensions were generated in SketchUp, reducing the chance of making a mistake when calculating and adding dimensions. Each piece shows an exploded view, along with conventional front, side, section and detail views. A few words about working with and interpreting the two-dimensional views is in order, as familiarity with mechanical drawing is not as common as it once was.

## Realities of Reading Drawings

Dimensions are shown in the views where they are most relevant, and not all parts are dimensioned in every view, nor are all possible dimensions included in every view. Understanding a piece of furniture takes time, and mechanical drawings require you to study all of the views thoroughly. To fully understand the construction, look at all the views and compare one to another. We're not trying to send you on a wild goose chase nor hiding important information; we're trying to ensure that you're not taking a glance at one drawing, making assumptions and heading for the saw.

To build any of these pieces, you'll need to spend time with the drawings, do some addition and subtraction and arrive at your own list of the parts needed. You'll have to decide how close to the finished dimensions you want to mill your material, what sub-assemblies you need to make, and how minor errors in dimensioning or making sub-assemblies will affect the size of other parts. This is part of the process of building furniture, and it's a good exercise to make sure that you understand how a piece goes together before you begin cutting wood and making parts.

Dimensions for doors and drawers are the actual sizes of the openings; you will need to decide what is an acceptable gap and adjust the sizes of the parts accordingly. One important detail to watch for is the relationship between lipped or overlay doors and drawers and their openings. In our drawings, the elevation view show the size of the finished front, including the overlay, and the section view shows larger detail with both the opening size and the amount of overlay. Look carefully at drawers; most of them are flush with the opening on the bottom and overlap the opening on the sides and top.

Two-dimensional views show parts accurately, but not realistically. In a front elevation, you see only width and height. The depth of objects in relation to one another can't be seen; you need to look at a side or top view to determine that. In addition to elevations, most of the pieces in this book include a section view. A section can be visualized by imagining a slice taken through the piece, showing the relationships of parts that would otherwise be hidden from view.

In these drawings, objects on the cutting plane are filled in with a grey color, and objects beyond the cutting plane are shown as solid lines. Sections show the relationships that aren't obvious in other points of view.

Detailed instructions of every step required to build the pieces from the drawings is beyond the scope of this book. The information about the sizes of all the parts is in the drawings, but you need to think about the sequence of assembling parts, and how sizes of other parts may change during building. For example, in a case piece the accepted practice is to put the carcase together, then fit moldings and feet to the case and build the drawers and doors to the sizes of the openings. This is how the original pieces were made.

The concept of cutting all parts to exact sizes before beginning construction is a product of the Industrial Revolution and assembly-line methods. It works, if you can maintain total control over the size and shape of each part, the wood doesn't move significantly in reaction to changes in humidity or moisture content as you build, and all of your sub-assemblies are perfect. When building one piece of furniture at a time, you're much better off to mill parts oversize, then trim and cut to an exact fit as you need a specific part. No one will notice if the finished piece of furniture is $1/16$" smaller overall than you intended, but a gap that size will be glaringly obvious.

If you lack experience, don't dive in and start building one of the large complex pieces in this book. Start with a smaller one so you don't waste a lot of material as you learn the process of planning and sequencing work. Read some general furniture-making books, such as Ernest Joyce's "The Encyclopedia of Furniture Making" (Sterling). Take a class and practice basic techniques to build your confidence. With a few small projects under your belt, you'll be equipped to make your masterpiece.

*A section view is often referred to as a cut. The visible parts of a section are on the cutting plane.*

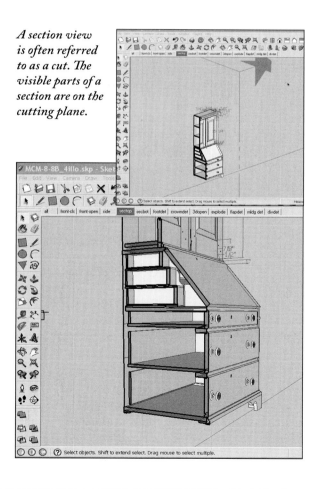

# Tables & Chairs

# Stretcher Table

*Built 1710–1725
in Charleston, South Carolina
of cypress, painted*

This form of table is a common one for the period, and the construction is similar to that of an English joint stool. The stretchers near the bottoms of the legs add structural strength, but do get in the way, as seen by the wear on this example. These tables had a wide range of uses, and are sometimes referred to as writing tables or toilette tables. Today as in the past, the usable but not-too-large work surface, accompanied by a drawer, suits many tasks without taking up a large amount of space.

The slender legs on this piece are more graceful than in many examples in the museum collection, and the rounded surfaces of the two-board top and lower stretchers add qualities of softness and femininity to the stout construction. This piece was painted blue when made, but it would also be attractive with a clear finish. A stand without a drawer, of similar construction and finish, is also in the MESDA collection.

## Minimal but Solid Construction

All of the joinery in the lower structure is pinned mortise-and-tenon joints; there are two pins where space allows and a single pin where the low stretchers and rail below the drawer enter the legs. The drawer supports are simply nailed to the aprons and fit within the legs. In the original, these were single pieces of wood, rabetted to support the drawer from below while restricting lateral movement. A modern maker might opt to use two pieces.

The drawer bottom on the original is three pieces butted side to side, with the grain running parallel to the drawer front. The bottom is nailed on from below, and the drawer rides directly on the bottom. The lower edge of the drawer front is rabetted to hide the edge of the bottom. This rabbet is shallower than the thickness of the bottom to provide a gap between the lower edge of the front and the top of the drawer rail. Two small blocks on the rear apron act as stops.

The top of the table is attached to the side and rear aprons of the table frame with wooden pegs driven in through the top surface. This was a common method during the period, but today this visible joinery would be frowned upon. There is some variation in the turnings. The pommels, where the square sections of the legs meet the round portions, appear to have been chamfered with a chisel after the legs were removed from the lathe.

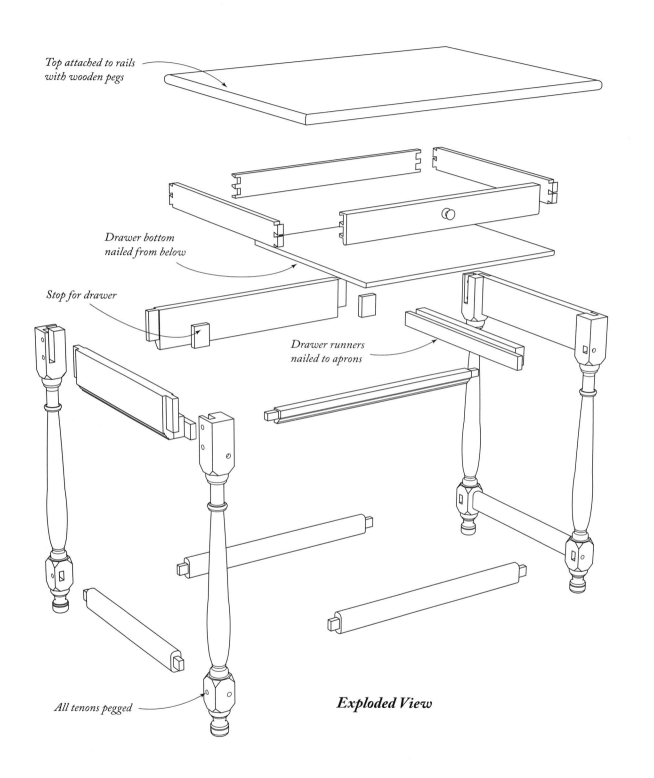

Top attached to rails
with wooden pegs

Drawer bottom
nailed from below

Stop for drawer

Drawer runners
nailed to aprons

All tenons pegged

**Exploded View**

MESDA COLLECTION, ACC. NO. 2457

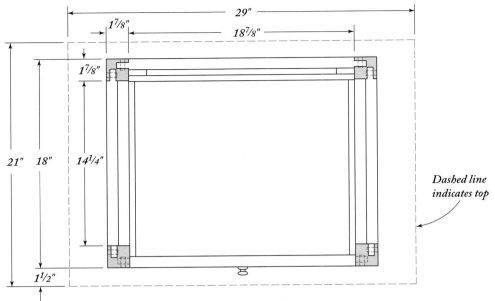

**Top – Section View**

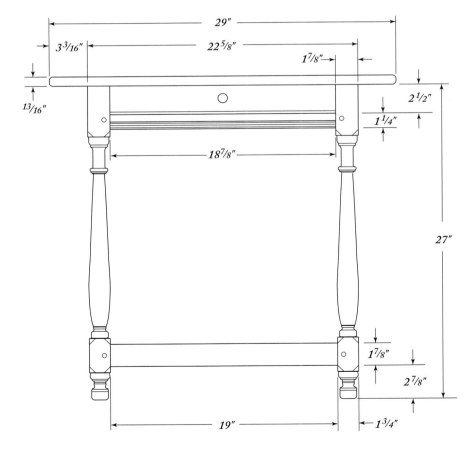

**Front View**

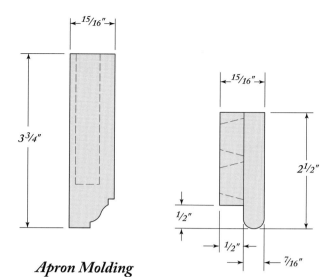

**Apron Molding**

**Drawer Front**

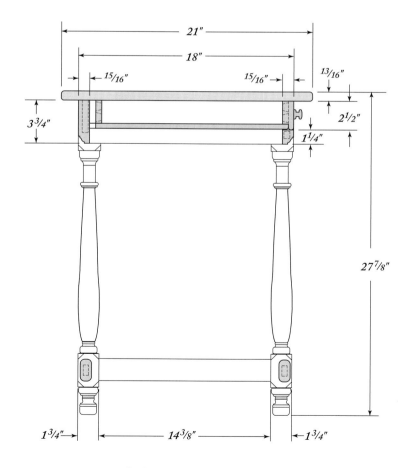

**Side – Section View**

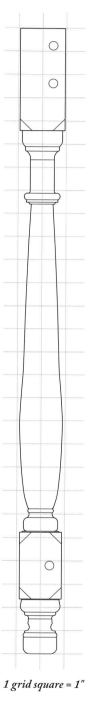

*1 grid square = 1"*

**Leg Pattern**

# Side Table

*Built circa 1805*
*most likely in Martinsburg, West Virginia*
*of walnut & poplar*

Attributed to John Shearer, this small walnut table has some interesting details, but there is a good chance that the poplar top is a replacement. The legs taper on all four sides to the spade feet, and there is a small reveal worked around the top of the feet. The arched aprons have a short, straight section at each terminus of the central arch. These types of details reflect the use of hand tools in forming them. There isn't a good way to handle these transitions with modern machinery, but they are vital to the character and charm of the piece.

The general form of the legs and aprons can be cut with a band saw, but the transitions where curves and lines meet should be worked carefully with chisel and gouge. The aprons are set in slightly from the legs, and the mortises are all pegged. This piece is in a private collection, so we don't know how the top is attached. The method of connecting the top will be up to the preferences of the builder. Pocket screws near the top of the aprons would be appropriate to the period, and the pockets can be formed with a chisel.

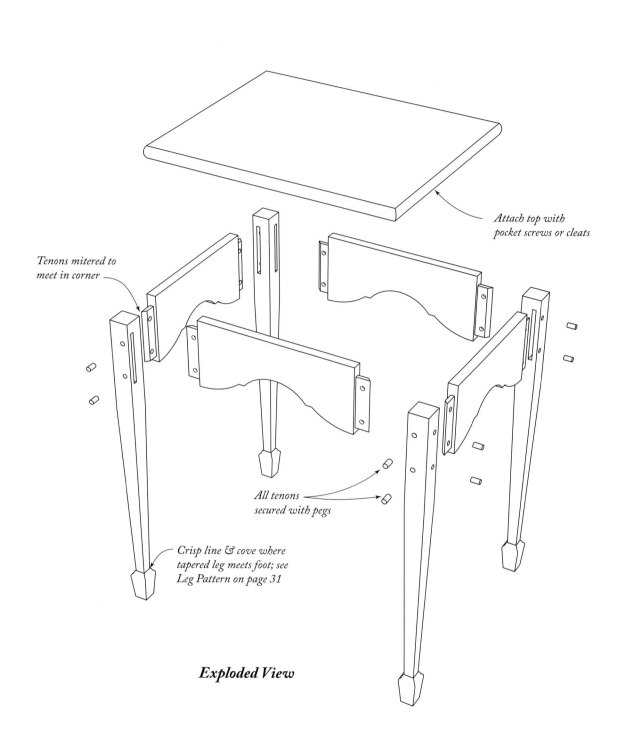

Attach top with
pocket screws or cleats

Tenons mitered to
meet in corner

All tenons
secured with pegs

Crisp line & cove where
tapered leg meets foot; see
Leg Pattern on page 31

**Exploded View**

MESDA RESEARCH FILE NO. 10,418

*Side Table*

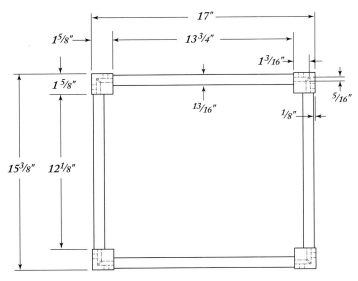

**Top View**

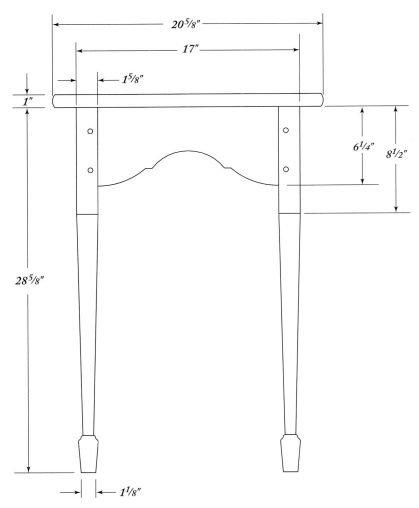

**Front View**

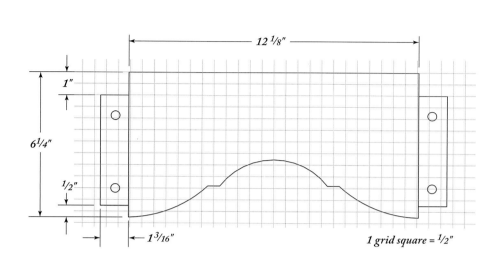

12 ⅛"

1"

6¼"

½"

1³/₁₆"

1 grid square = ½"

**Side Apron Pattern**

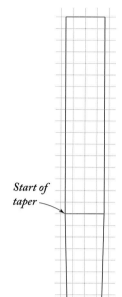

Start of taper

1 grid square = ½"

**Leg Pattern**

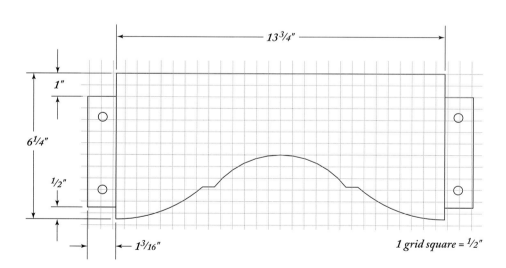

13¾"

1"

6¼"

½"

1³/₁₆"

1 grid square = ½"

**Front & Back Apron Pattern**

# Pad-foot Table

❦

*Built 1765–1790*
*in the Roanoke River Basin of North Carolina*
*of walnut, poplar & yellow pine*

This form of table was popular in the American South, as well as in England, for an extended period of time. This example serves as evidence that early Southern furniture made near the coast was typically far from rustic and not lacking in attention to detail. The cove at the bottom of the feet was unique to the Roanoke River Basin of North Carolina. The legs are turned from two centers at the bottom, which allows the legs to taper in to the back of the feet.

The decorative scallops at the corners of the top and molded outer corners of the upper legs add a sophisticated touch. Similar in size, shape and configuration to the Stretcher Table that opens this section, this type of table suited many purposes and would be found in various rooms.

Typical of the period, the drawer runners were simply nailed to the inside of the aprons, as were the kickers at the top of the drawer that serve double-duty as supports for the top. Screws from below through the kickers hold the top to the base, along with pocket screws in the back apron and front upper rail.

The drawer sides, back and bottom are all made from poplar; the bottom is beveled on three sides and fits in grooves in the front and sides. The drawer supports within the aprons are yellow pine, and the knob is of cast pewter, clinched inside the drawer front.

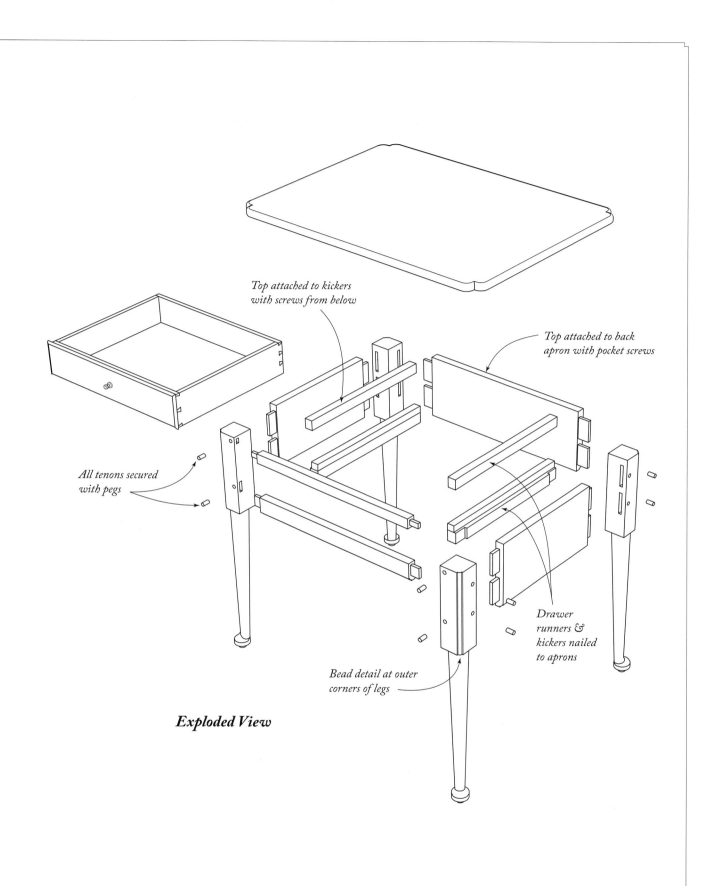

Top attached to kickers
with screws from below

Top attached to back
apron with pocket screws

All tenons secured
with pegs

Drawer
runners &
kickers nailed
to aprons

Bead detail at outer
corners of legs

**Exploded View**

MESDA COLLECTION, ACC. NO. 2805

*Pad-foot Table*

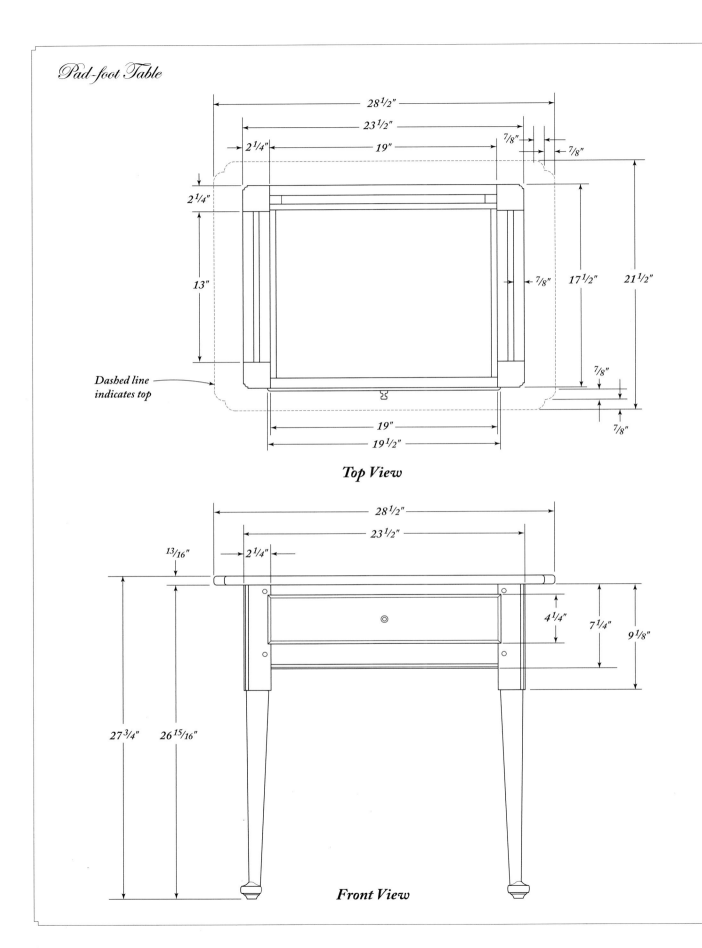

**Top View**

Dashed line
indicates top

28¹/₂"
23¹/₂"
2¹/₄"   19"   ⁷/₈"   ⁷/₈"
2¹/₄"
13"   ⁷/₈"   17¹/₂"   21¹/₂"
⁷/₈"
19"   ⁷/₈"
19¹/₂"

**Front View**

28¹/₂"
23¹/₂"
13/16"   2¹/₄"
4¹/₄"   7¹/₄"   9¹/₈"
27³/₄"   26¹⁵/₁₆"

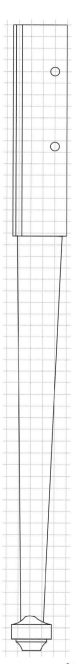

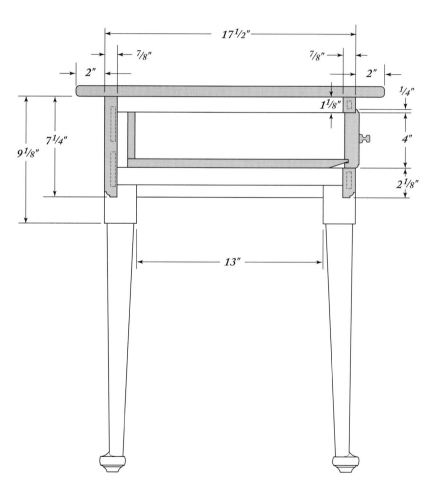

**Side – Section View**

*1 grid square = ¹/₂"*

**Leg Pattern**

# Work Table

*Built in Salem, North Carolina
of tiger maple & poplar*

The settlement at Salem was a group of Moravians with close ties to Southern Pennsylvania. They were obsessive record keepers, and most of the original buildings are intact and exist today as Old Salem Museums & Gardens. Numerous pieces of period Salem furniture are intact as well. Some Moravian pieces can be easily mistaken for Pennsylvanian. This small table is one of the few pieces in this book not made of walnut, and the choice of tiger maple for the primary wood may be a reflection of the Moravian connection to the North. Unfortunately, we don't know when this piece was built.

Poplar was the secondary, interior wood, and the glass knobs are replacements. In all probability the original pulls were round wooden knobs, similar to what we show in the drawings. Circular outlines of the old knobs are visible on the drawer fronts.

The top drawer is divided into six sections, suggesting that this table was used for sewing or other small work. The drawer fronts have a slight bead worked around the perimeter, and this bead detail is also found along the length of the lower edges of the side and back aprons.

The transition between the square section of the legs and the turned portion is rather abrupt to modern eyes, but this detail reflects the times.

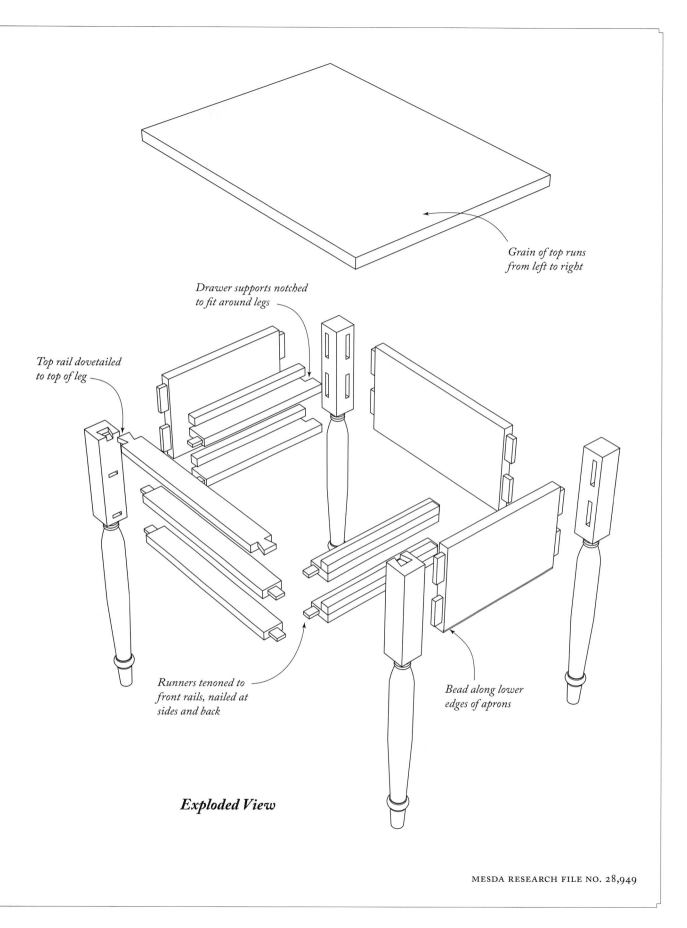

Grain of top runs
from left to right

Drawer supports notched
to fit around legs

Top rail dovetailed
to top of leg

Runners tenoned to
front rails, nailed at
sides and back

Bead along lower
edges of aprons

**Exploded View**

MESDA RESEARCH FILE NO. 28,949

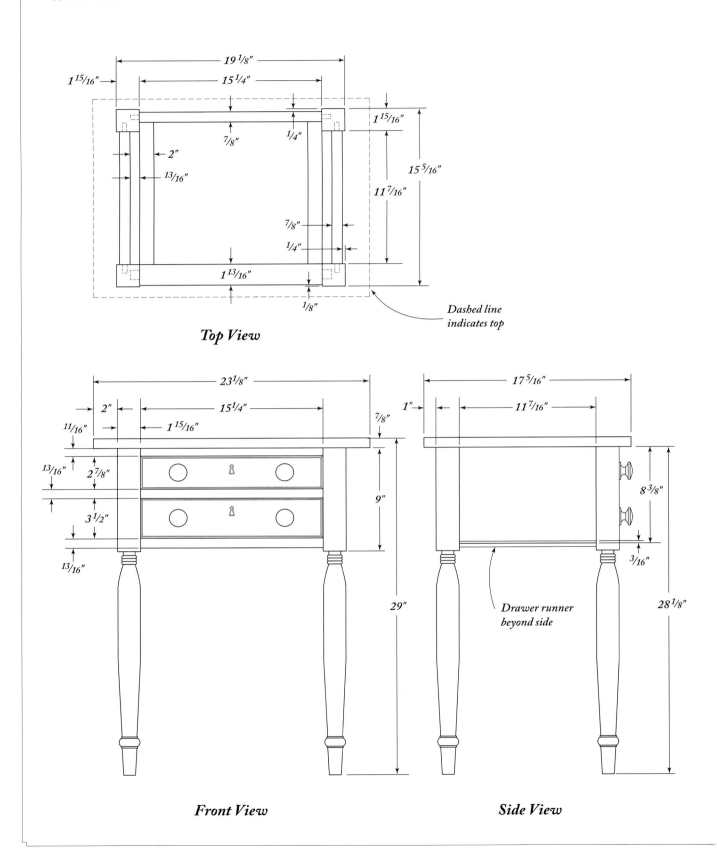

**Top View**

Dashed line indicates top

**Front View**

**Side View**

Drawer runner beyond side

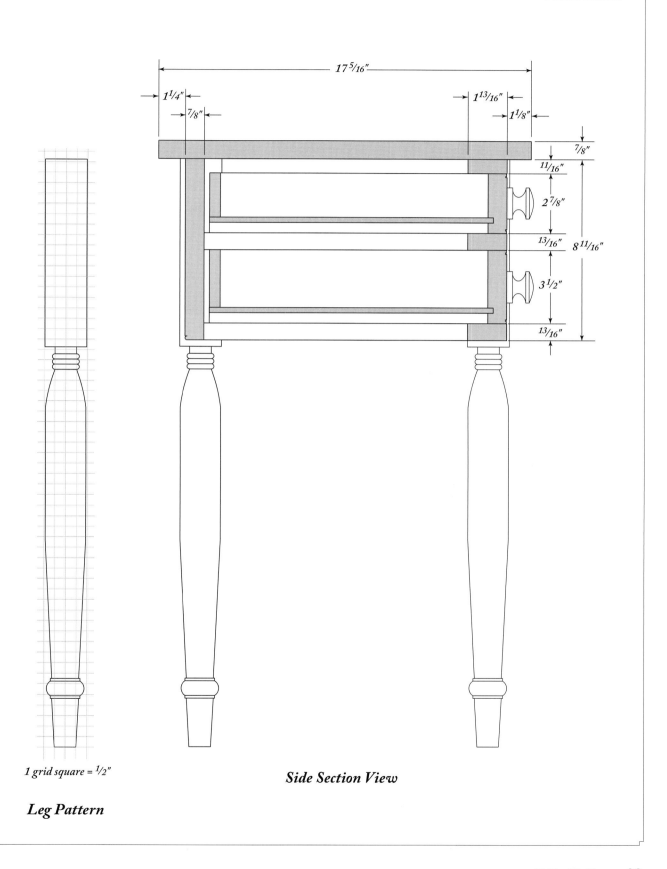

$17^{5/16}$"

$1^{1/4}$"

$7/8$"

$1^{13/16}$"

$1^{1/8}$"

$7/8$"

$11/16$"

$2^{7/8}$"

$13/16$"

$8^{11/16}$"

$3^{1/2}$"

$13/16$"

*1 grid square = $^{1}/_{2}$"*

**Side Section View**

**Leg Pattern**

# Stand

*Built 1800–1810*
*most likely in the Valley of Virginia*
*of walnut & yellow pine*

Today we tend to think of small stands such as this one as display pieces for a plant or perhaps a piece of art. In the early 19th century this piece's purpose was utilitarian; it was intended to hold a wash bowl or basin. In either case, this is an attractive piece and the use of thin legs and stock gives it a delicate appearance. That delicacy provides some challenges when it comes to joinery.

This piece is part of a private collection, so we prepared the drawings from a single photograph and brief examiner's description. The joinery shown in the drawings is our conjecture, and if you build one of these stands you will need to make the same decisions we made when creating the drawings, and the original builder made some 200 years ago.

## Joinery Compromise

There isn't much material in the legs to accommodate tenons coming from two directions. This lack of space puts the builder in the position of violating the rules of sound joinery in some way. Our choice was to allow the mortises to intersect, make the tenons as long as possible, and to cut the ends of the tenons back at an angle so they don't interfere with each other. This cut is the same as it would be for a 45° miter joint, but the ends of the tenons should not meet. A small gap will ensure that the shoulders of the tenons may be held tight to the legs.

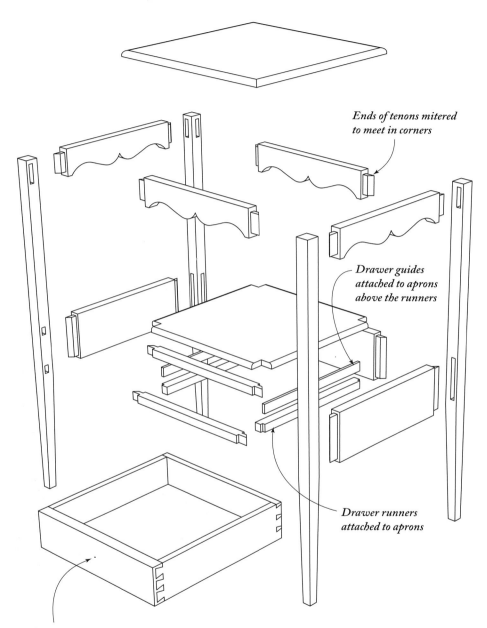

Ends of tenons mitered
to meet in corners

Drawer guides
attached to aprons
above the runners

Drawer runners
attached to aprons

Drawer pull is missing from original; no indication
as to what pull or knob was used

**Exploded View**

MESDA RESEARCH FILE NO. 7,423

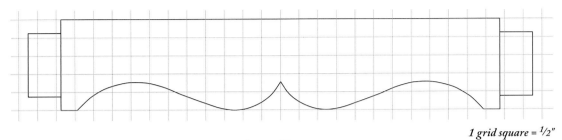

**Apron Pattern**

*1 grid square = ¹/₂"*

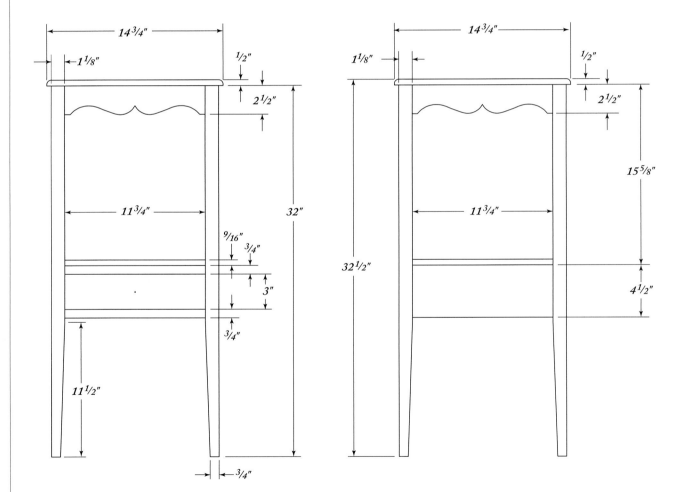

**Front View**                    **Side View**

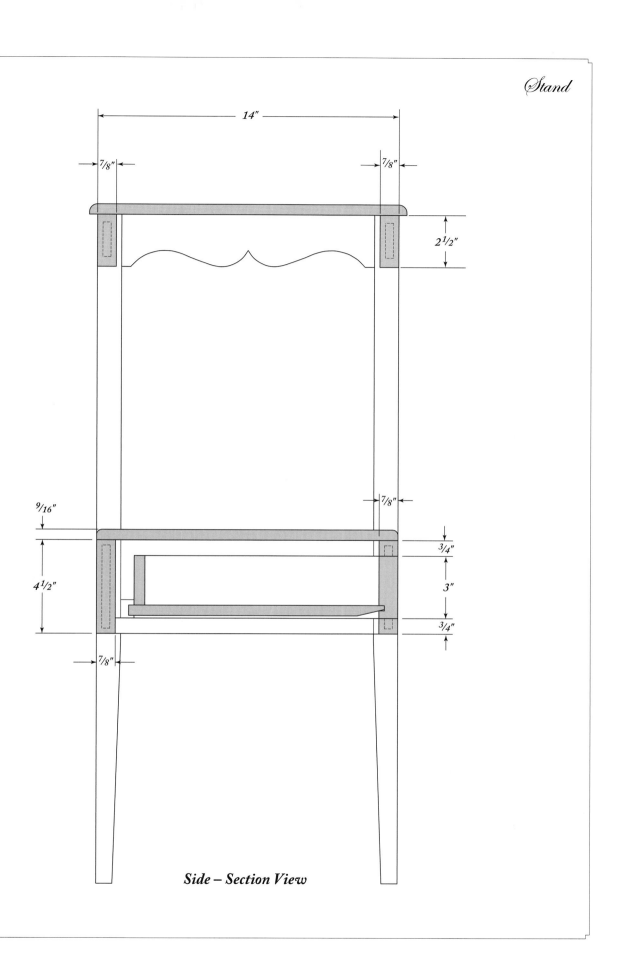

14"

7/8"                    7/8"

2 1/2"

9/16"                                        7/8"

3/4"

4 1/2"                                3"

3/4"

7/8"

***Side – Section View***

# Pembroke Table

*Built 1800–1820*
*by Peter Eddleman*
*in Lincoln County, North Carolina*
*of walnut, yellow pine & maple with light wood inlay*

Drop-leaf tables, commonly called Pembroke tables, are an iconic Southern furniture form. This example, from the Southwestern North Carolina Piedmont, has the typical appearance of a high-style table, but maker Peter Eddleman had his own methods of adding inlay. Instead of strips of patterned veneers let into a groove, the inlay patterns on this table are small individual pieces, each let directly into the solid-wood top.

This blend of urban detail and rural execution is found in many pieces of early Southern furniture. An awareness of current styles shows that there was a connection between city and country at the time. This connection may well have been in the form of a wealthy customer describing details seen on a trip to the city. While the rural cabinetmaker had a sense of how the finished piece ought to look, he often relied on his own devices and ingenuity for accomplishing the task.

The drawings for this piece were prepared from photographs, and the detail of the support mechanism for the leaves is an educated guess on our part. It is based on other examples in the MESDA collection, and is typical of the period. Essentially a wooden hinge, the support bracket is beveled on the hidden

side to make it easy to grip when swinging it into position to support the leaf.

Tables of this type were made in many sizes, and served as decorative side tables that could be pressed into service to provide extra seating when company came for gaming or dining.

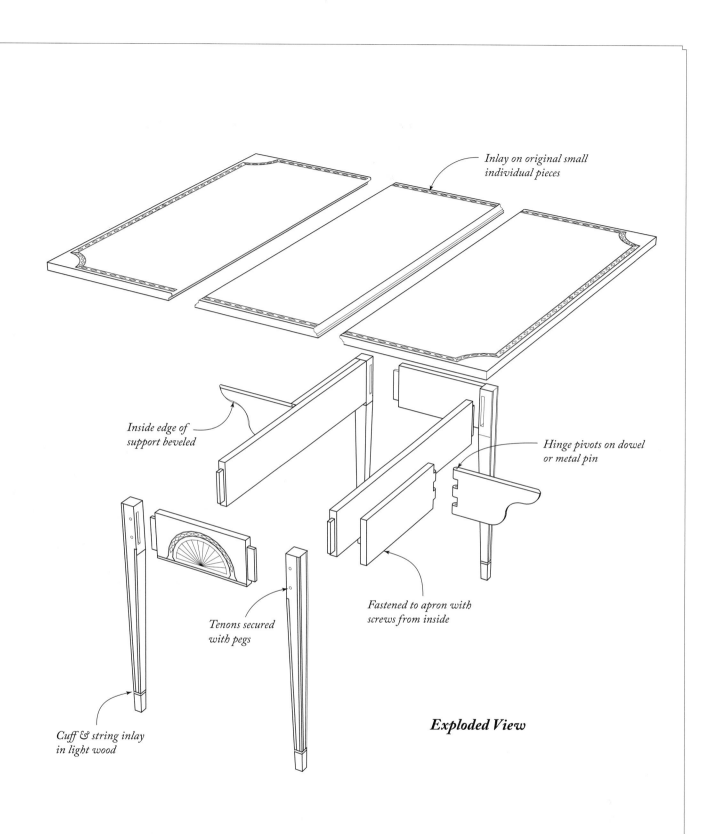

Inlay on original small
individual pieces

Inside edge of
support beveled

Hinge pivots on dowel
or metal pin

Tenons secured
with pegs

Fastened to apron with
screws from inside

**Exploded View**

Cuff & string inlay
in light wood

MESDA COLLECTION, ACC. NO. 2073.26

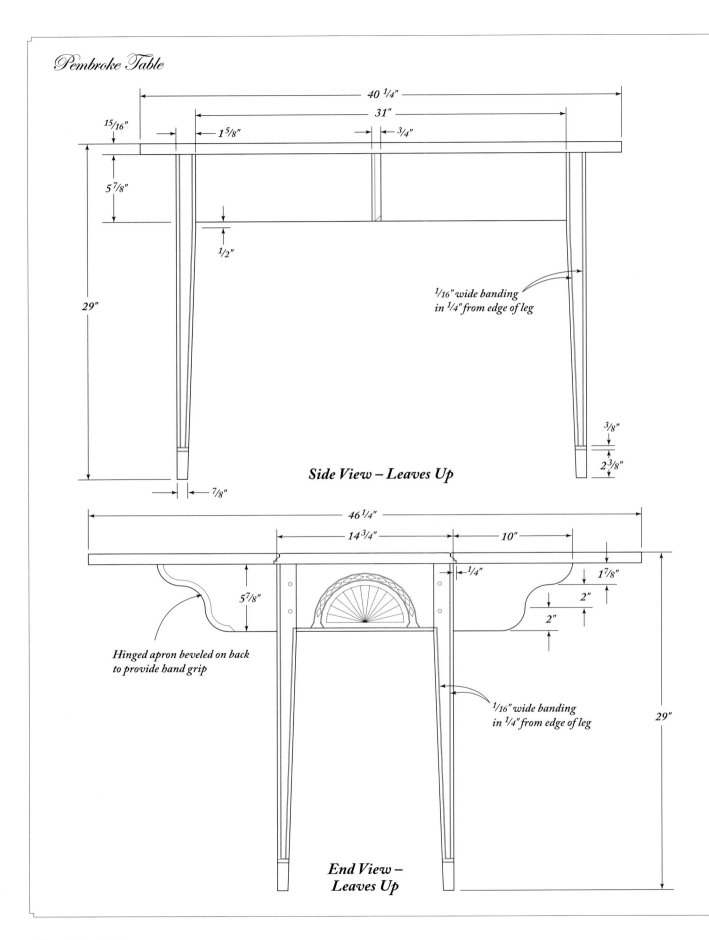

Pembroke Table

40 1/4"

31"

15/16"

1 5/8"        3/4"

5 7/8"

1/2"

1/16" wide banding
in 1/4" from edge of leg

29"

3/8"

2 3/8"

**Side View – Leaves Up**

7/8"

46 1/4"

14 3/4"              10"

1/4"

1 7/8"

5 7/8"

2"

2"

Hinged apron beveled on back
to provide hand grip

1/16" wide banding
in 1/4" from edge of leg

29"

**End View –
Leaves Up**

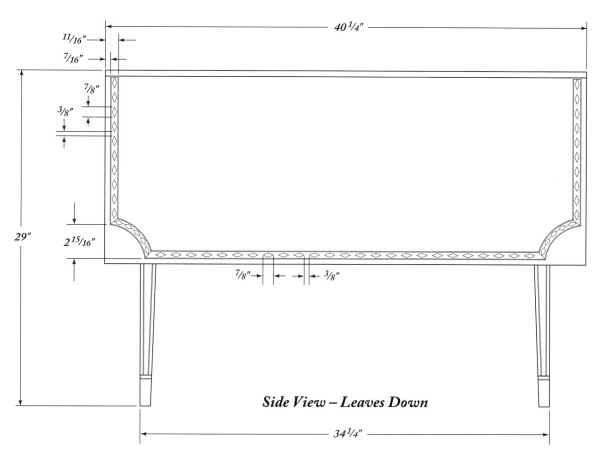

40 1/4"

11/16"

7/16"

7/8"

3/8"

29"

2 15/16"

7/8"   3/8"

**Side View – Leaves Down**

34 1/4"

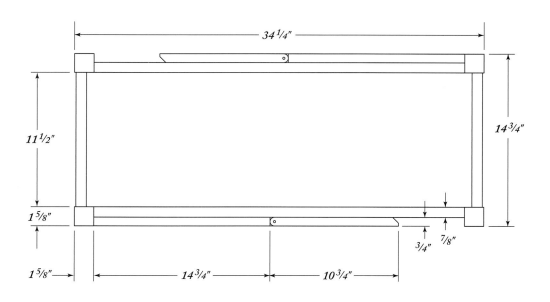

34 1/4"

11 1/2"

14 3/4"

1 5/8"

3/4"   7/8"

1 5/8"   14 3/4"   10 3/4"

**Base – Top View**

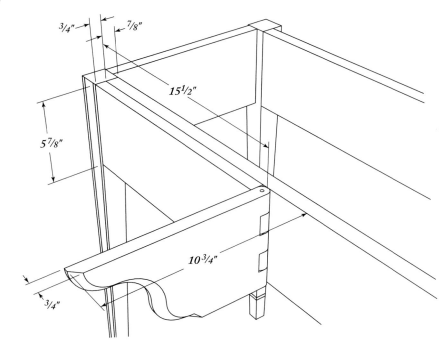

3/4"   7/8"

15¹/₂"

5⁷/₈"

10³/₄"

3/4"

**Support Detail**

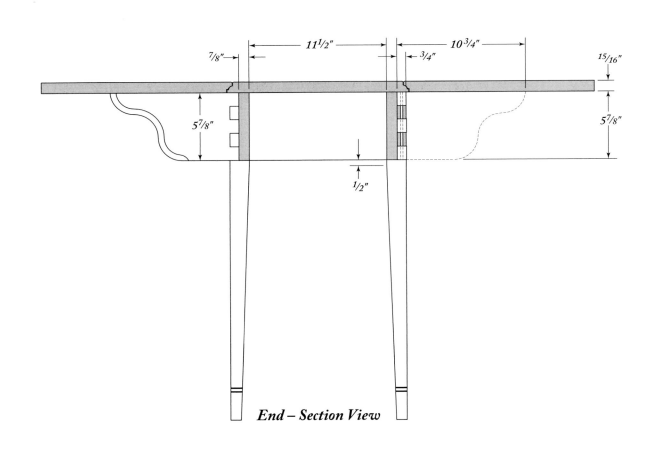

7/8"   11¹/₂"   10³/₄"   15/16"

3/4"

5⁷/₈"   5⁷/₈"

¹/₂"

**End – Section View**

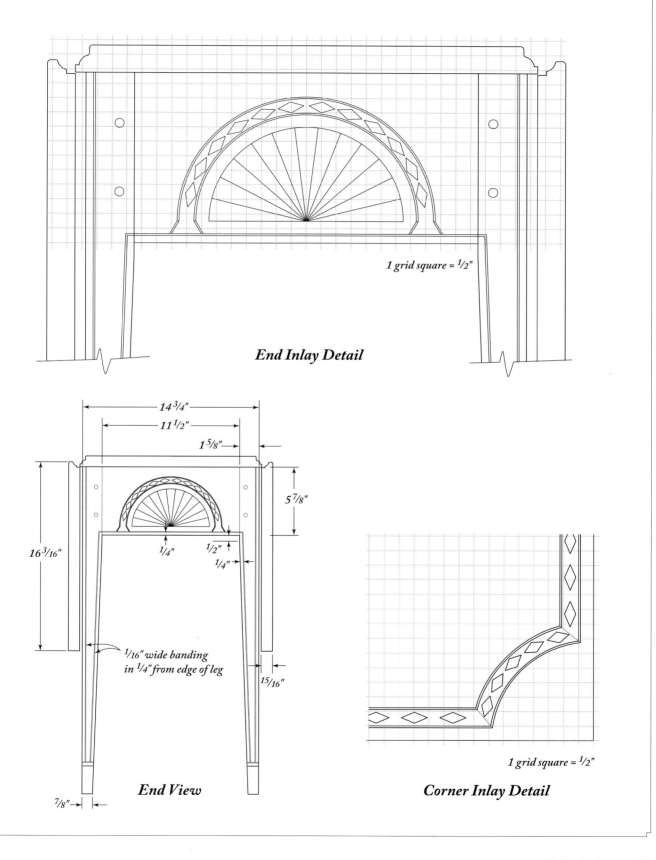

*1 grid square = ¹/₂"*

**End Inlay Detail**

14³/₄"

11¹/₂"

1⁵/₈"

5⁷/₈"

16³/₁₆"

¹/₄"   ¹/₂"

¹/₄"

¹/₁₆" *wide banding
in* ¹/₄" *from edge of leg*

15/16"

7/8"

**End View**

*1 grid square = ¹/₂"*

**Corner Inlay Detail**

# *Side Chair*

*Built 1769
in Winchester, Virginia
of walnut with a split oak seat*

Southern furniture makers worked under many influences, reflecting the diverse culture of the early American South. Museum notes for this chair mention Chinese, English, German and Moravian design elements. The northern end of the Shenandoah Valley was in the country, but was a crossroads for migration in the mid-1700s, and this chair is an interesting blend of the stylistic and structural elements that were present in the period.

In a rural area, woodworkers often combined facets of the trade that would be separated in a more urban setting. In this case the addition of some turned elements in an otherwise joined square construction leads to the conclusion that the maker of this chair was comfortable with turning, but wasn't in the business of making turned chairs. Many of the other pieces in this book have turned details, something a cabinetmaker without a lathe (or a need for one) wouldn't likely add.

The split oak seat is a separate piece, a "slip seat" that is woven around a wood frame and rests within the seat rails of the chair frame. The mortise-and-tenon construction yields a solid chair, and the tenons on the back end of the seat side rails pierce the back legs, and terminate in a decorative detail. Most of the joints are secured with two pegs, located close to the outer limits of the tenons.

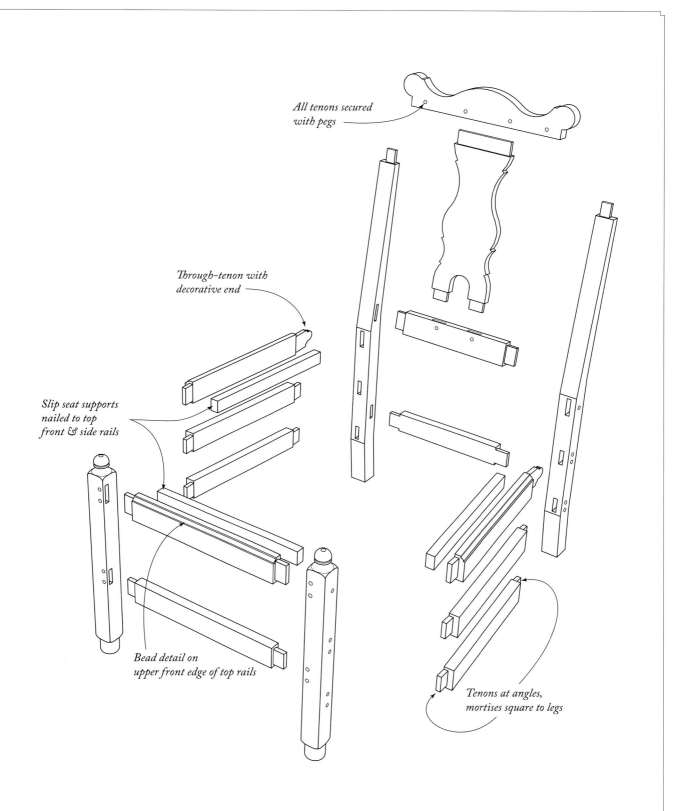

All tenons secured
with pegs

Through-tenon with
decorative end

Slip seat supports
nailed to top
front & side rails

Bead detail on
upper front edge of top rails

Tenons at angles,
mortises square to legs

**Exploded View**

MESDA COLLECTION, ACC. NO. 2424

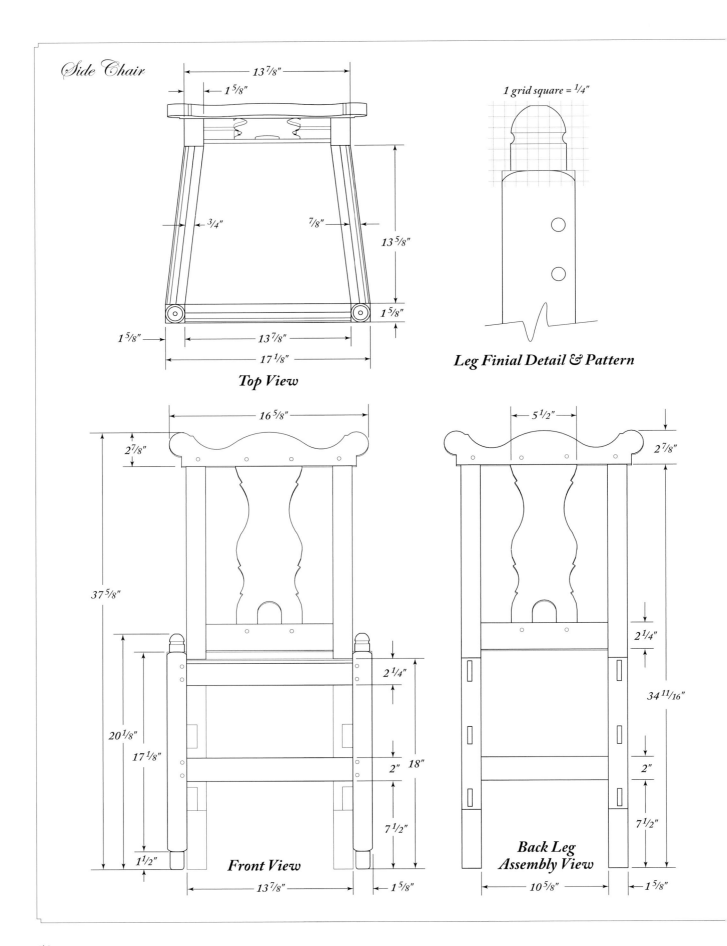

*Side Chair*

13 7/8"

1 5/8"

3/4"   7/8"

13 5/8"

1 5/8"

1 5/8"

13 7/8"

17 1/8"

**Top View**

1 grid square = 1/4"

**Leg Finial Detail & Pattern**

16 5/8"

2 7/8"

5 1/2"

2 7/8"

37 5/8"

2 1/4"

34 11/16"

20 1/8"

17 1/8"

2 1/4"

2"   18"

2"

7 1/2"

7 1/2"

1 1/2"

**Front View**

13 7/8"   1 5/8"

**Back Leg Assembly View**

10 5/8"   1 5/8"

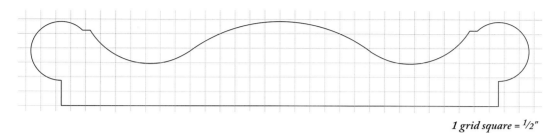

**Back Crest Rail Pattern**

*1 grid square = ¹/₂"*

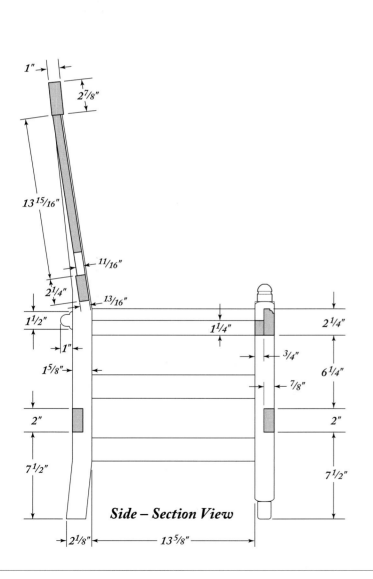

1"

2⁷/₈"

13¹⁵/₁₆"

¹¹/₁₆"

2¹/₄"

¹³/₁₆"

1¹/₂"

1"

1⁵/₈"

2"

7¹/₂"

1¹/₄"

³/₄"

⁷/₈"

2¹/₄"

6¹/₄"

2"

7¹/₂"

**Side – Section View**

2¹/₈"    13⁵/₈"

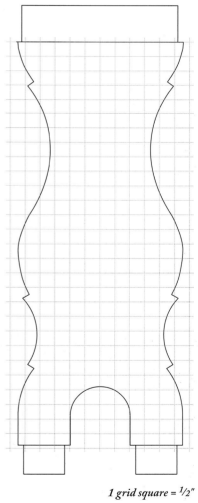

**Back Splat Pattern**

*1 grid square = ¹/₂"*

# Case Pieces

# Desk with Bookcase

Built 1775-1790
in Salem, North Carolina
by Johannes Krause
of walnut & yellow pine

*J*ohannes Krause was the master cabinetmaker in Salem in the latter part of the 1700s, and in addition to managing the joiners' shop and training apprentices, he took charge of many other construction-related tasks in the village. Probably trained in Europe, Krause built several similar desks; many of them are still located in Old Salem. Demanding of his apprentices, he made solid furniture but the people of the community condemned his lifestyle. He eventually was asked to leave the area on account of his behavior.

These desks apparently were a status symbol in Salem, and Krause had the proportions and details down to a science. Bracket feet can be a weak point in this type of furniture, but he found the ideal configuration of height, shape and corner-block placement. Also noteworthy is the relative simplicity of the desk interior. Most surviving examples have the simple shelf seen here as opposed to the fancy prospects and hidden compartments seen in similar pieces made in the North.

Krause's style also featured distinctive moldings, such as the deeply cut cove in the cornice, and the small fillet around the door panels. Moravian pieces tended to use thicker and wider stock, adding to the solid stance and helping to ensure the longevity of the furniture of Salem.

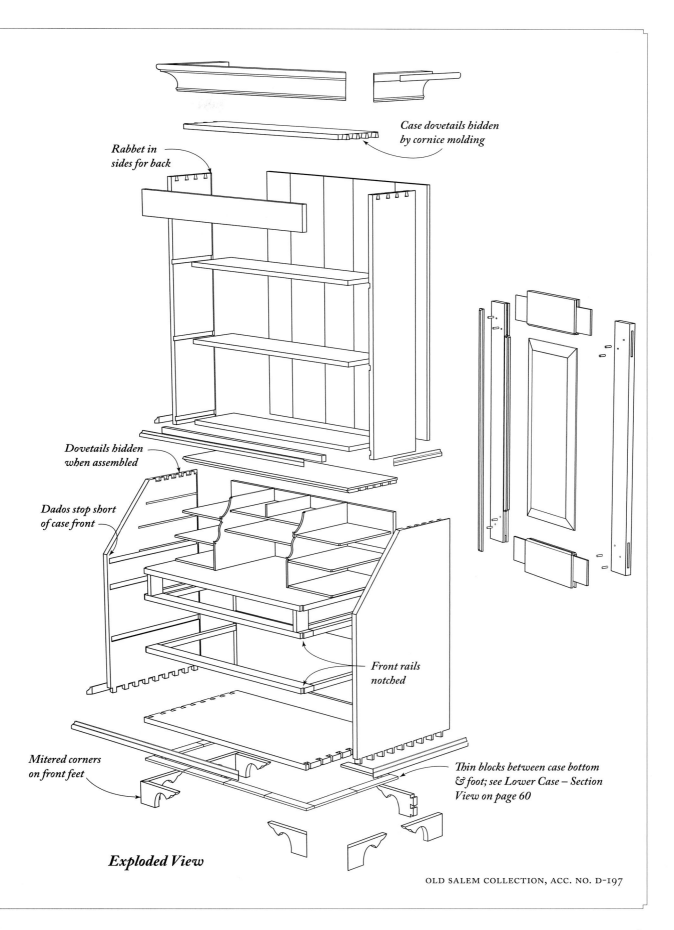

Case dovetails hidden
by cornice molding

*Rabbet in
sides for back*

*Dovetails hidden
when assembled*

*Dados stop short
of case front*

*Front rails
notched*

*Mitered corners
on front feet*

Thin blocks between case bottom
& foot; see Lower Case – Section
View on page 60

**Exploded View**

OLD SALEM COLLECTION, ACC. NO. D-197

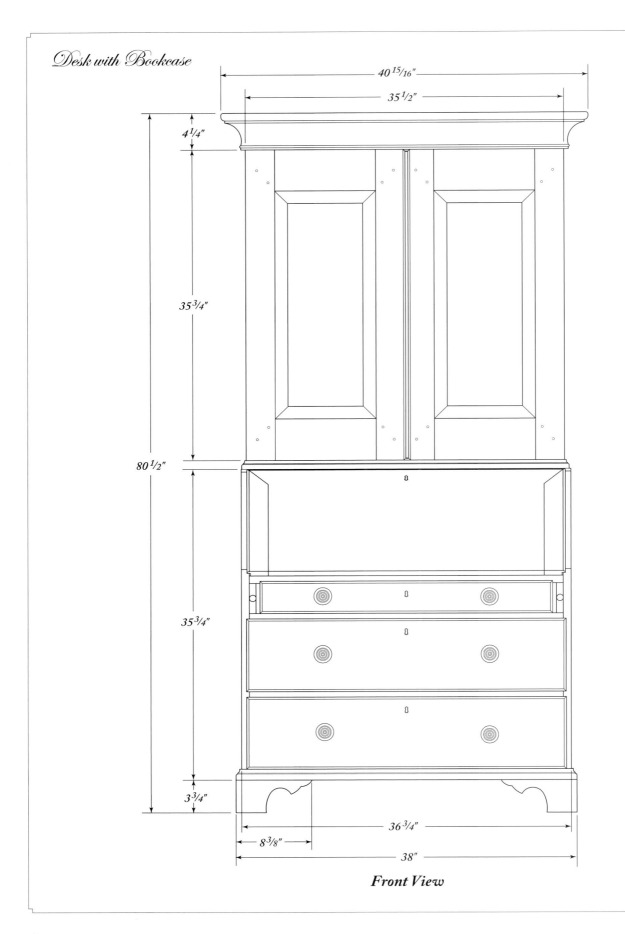

*Desk with Bookcase*

40 $^{15}/_{16}$"

35 $^1/_2$"

4 $^1/_4$"

35 $^3/_4$"

80 $^1/_2$"

35 $^3/_4$"

3 $^3/_4$"

36 $^3/_4$"

8 $^3/_8$"

38"

**Front View**

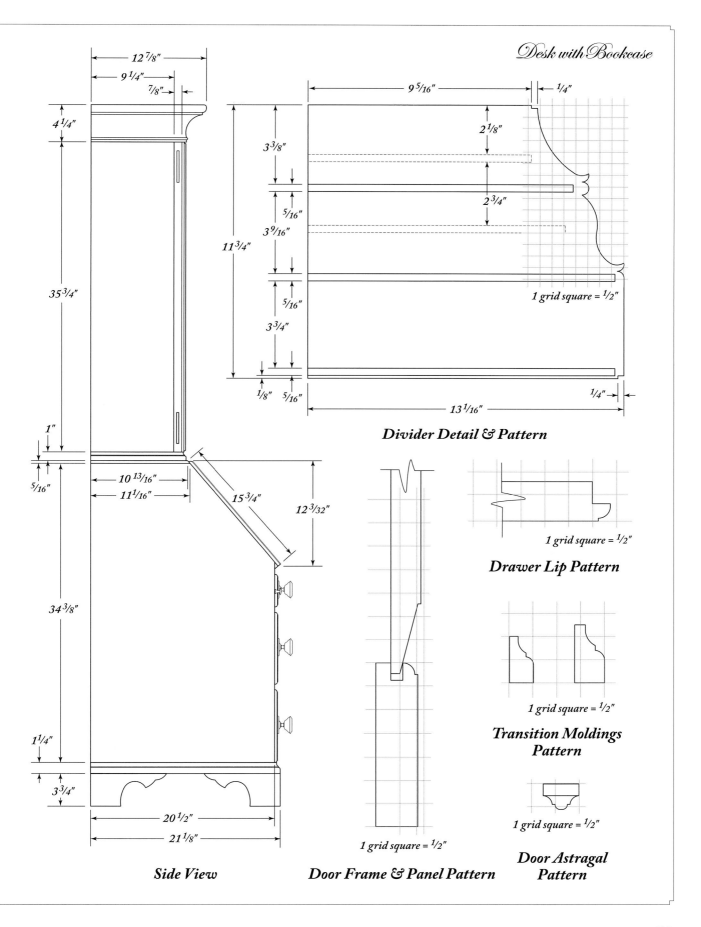

12 ⁷/₈"

9 ¹/₄"

⁷/₈"

4 ¹/₄"

35 ³/₄"

11 ³/₄"

9 ⁵/₁₆"

¹/₄"

2 ¹/₈"

3 ³/₈"

5/₁₆"

3 ⁹/₁₆"

2 ³/₄"

5/₁₆"

3 ³/₄"

¹/₈"

5/₁₆"

¹/₄"

13 ¹/₁₆"

*1 grid square = ¹/₂"*

**Divider Detail & Pattern**

1"

5/₁₆"

10 ¹³/₁₆"

11 ¹/₁₆"

15 ³/₄"

12 ³/₃₂"

34 ³/₈"

1 ¹/₄"

3 ³/₄"

20 ¹/₂"

21 ¹/₈"

**Side View**

**Door Frame & Panel Pattern**

*1 grid square = ¹/₂"*

*1 grid square = ¹/₂"*

**Drawer Lip Pattern**

*1 grid square = ¹/₂"*

**Transition Moldings Pattern**

*1 grid square = ¹/₂"*

**Door Astragal Pattern**

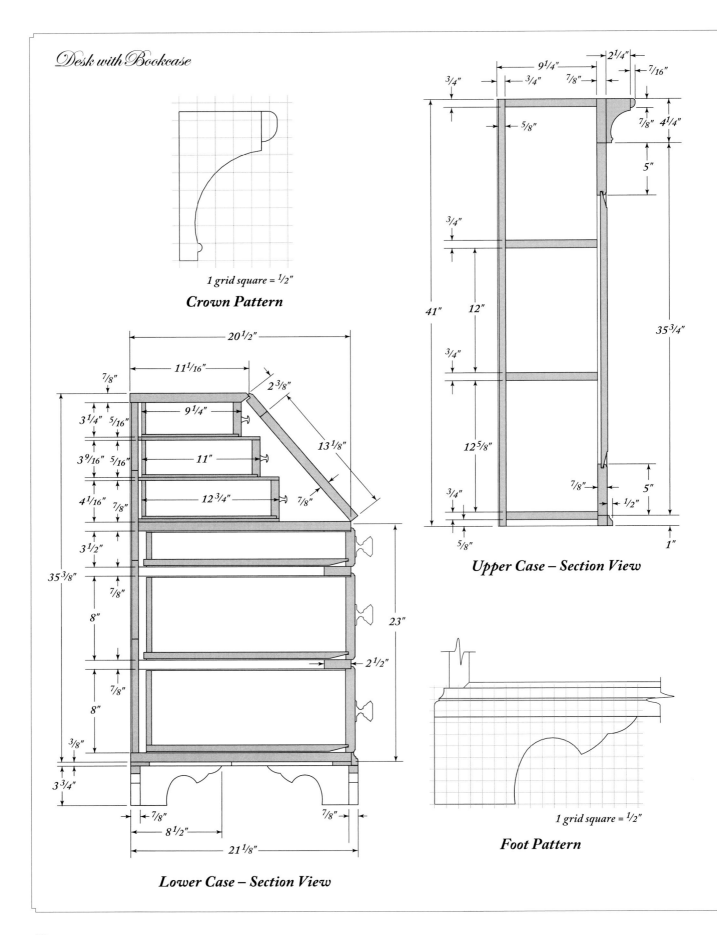

**Crown Pattern**

*1 grid square = ¹/₂"*

**Upper Case – Section View**

**Lower Case – Section View**

**Foot Pattern**

*1 grid square = ¹/₂"*

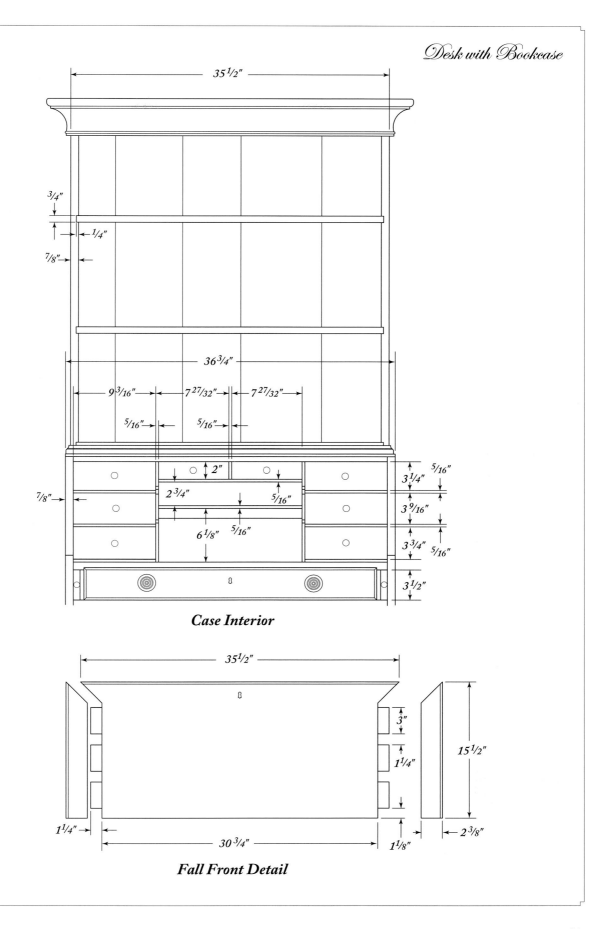

**Case Interior**

**Fall Front Detail**

# Cupboard

*Built in the Piedmont Region of North Carolina of walnut & yellow pine*

**M**onumental in size and appearance, this piece would be a challenge to move because it is constructed in one piece. While the scrollwork is ornate, the joinery is relatively simple; the horizontal parts are dadoed into the one-piece sides and are nailed from the outside of the case.

The face frame is nailed on to the front of the case, as are the boards of the back. The backboards overlay the case sides leaving the edges visible from the outside. The drawer bottoms are nailed to the drawer sides and back, and fit in a rabbet at the bottom of the drawer front.

The wide walnut planks used in this piece were common more than a century ago, but are extremely rare today. Yellow pine is used for the drawer boxes and the frame on which the drawers slide. Pivoting wooden catches keep the doors closed, and the doors are hung on simple wrought iron rattail hinges.

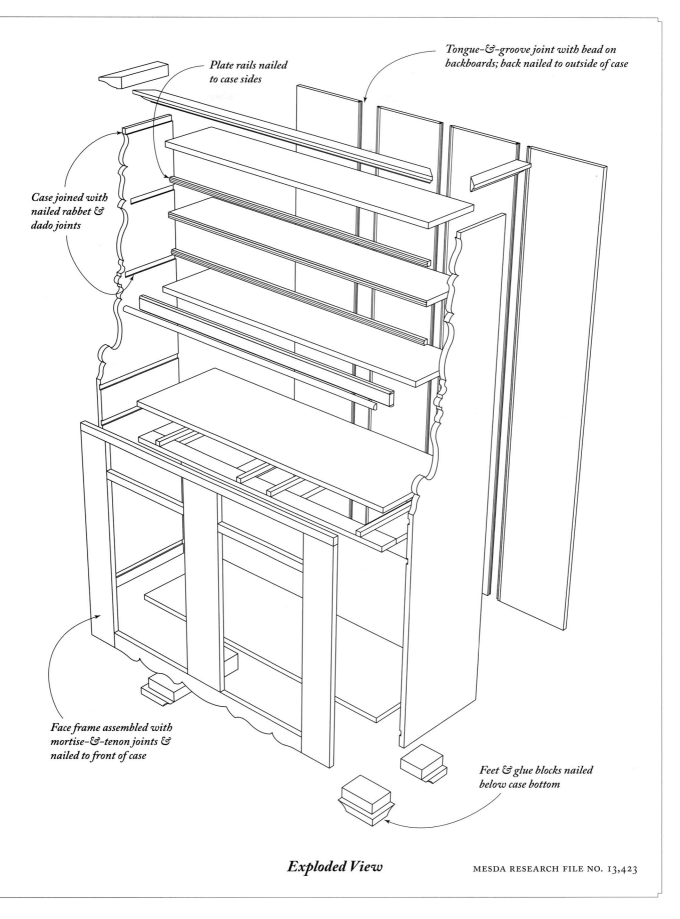

Tongue-&-groove joint with bead on
backboards; back nailed to outside of case

Plate rails nailed
to case sides

Case joined with
nailed rabbet &
dado joints

Face frame assembled with
mortise-&-tenon joints &
nailed to front of case

Feet & glue blocks nailed
below case bottom

**Exploded View**

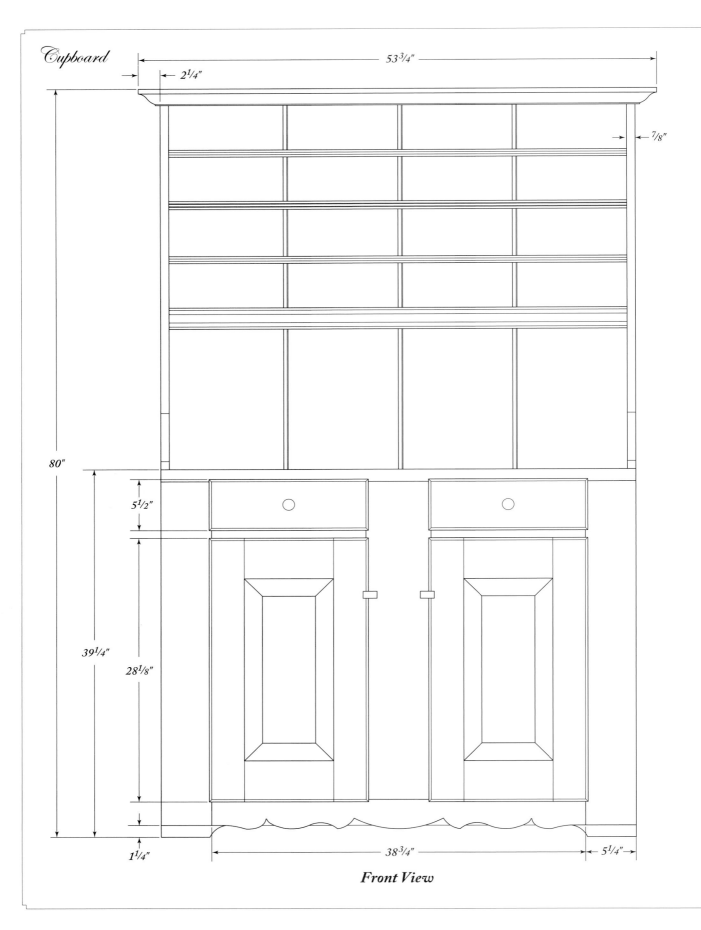

*Cupboard*

53³/₄"

2¹/₄"

⁷/₈"

80"

5¹/₂"

39¹/₄"

28¹/₈"

1¹/₄"

38³/₄"

5¹/₄"

**Front View**

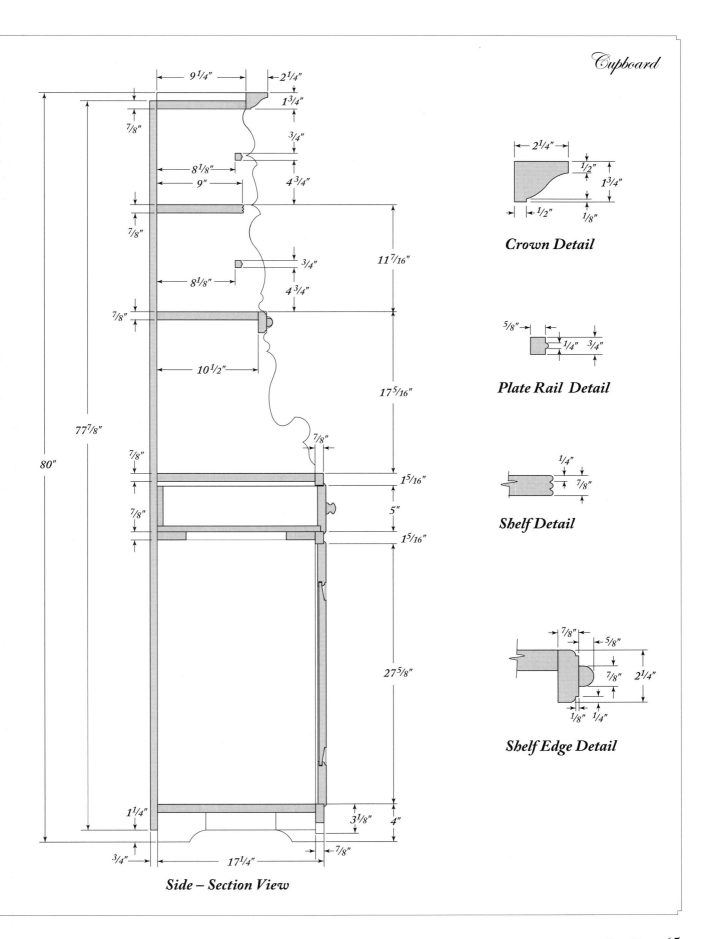

**Crown Detail**

**Plate Rail Detail**

**Shelf Detail**

**Shelf Edge Detail**

**Side – Section View**

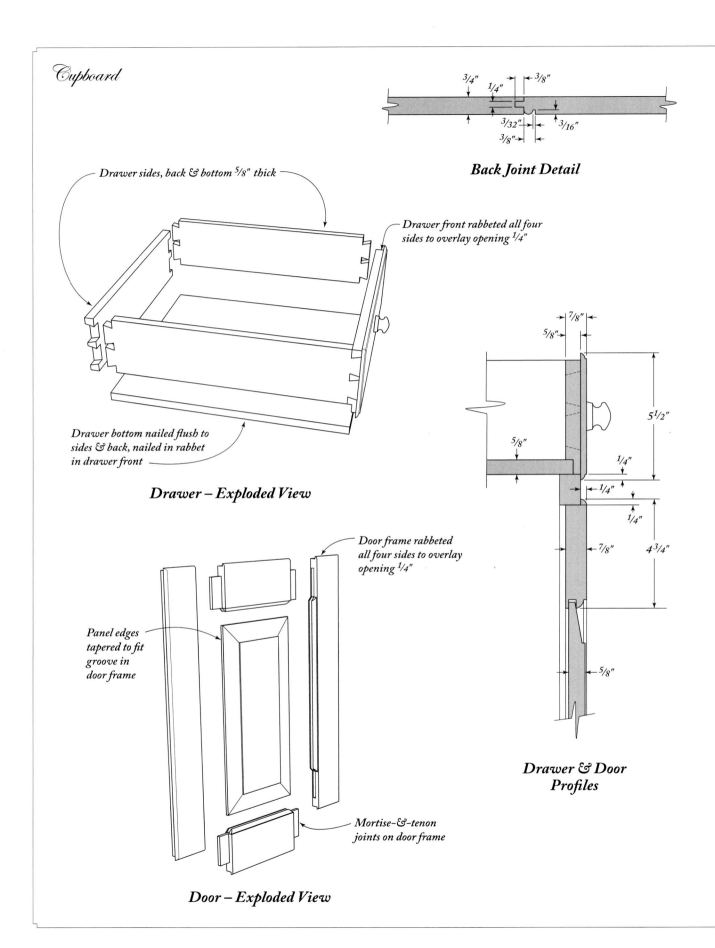

**Back Joint Detail**

3/4"   1/4"   3/8"

3/32"   3/16"

3/8"

*Drawer sides, back & bottom 5/8" thick*

*Drawer front rabbeted all four sides to overlay opening 1/4"*

*Drawer bottom nailed flush to sides & back, nailed in rabbet in drawer front*

**Drawer – Exploded View**

7/8"

5/8"

5/8"

5/8"

1/4"

1/4"

1/4"

7/8"

5 1/2"

4 3/4"

5/8"

**Drawer & Door Profiles**

*Door frame rabbeted all four sides to overlay opening 1/4"*

*Panel edges tapered to fit groove in door frame*

*Mortise-&-tenon joints on door frame*

**Door – Exploded View**

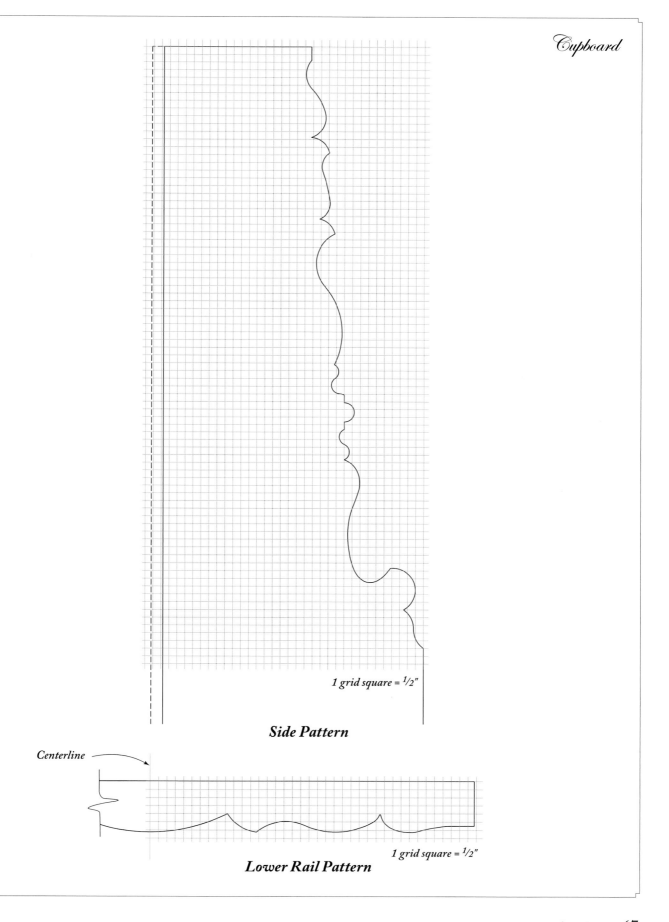

*1 grid square = ¹/₂"*

**Side Pattern**

Centerline

*1 grid square = ¹/₂"*

**Lower Rail Pattern**

# *Kitchen Press*

*Built 1790–1820
in Montgomery or possibly
Randolph County, North Carolina
of yellow pine & poplar, painted*

The painted finish of this piece, arched doors and overall proportions speak of German origins and influences. The main color is a muted red, with black and white accents. The band of half-round dentil molding at the cornice repeats each of the three colors. The front of the base between the feet drops a few inches on each side to meet in a central V shape.

The cupboard, or press, is so well proportioned that it is difficult to tell its size without context. Like many old pieces it is quite large, just more than 7' high by 4' wide. For all of its visual sophistication, there are a few places where the builder made some details in unusual ways, then had to come up with some creative solutions to finish the job.

## Where Moldings Meet

The dentil molding presents a layout challenge in finding an ideal size and number of repetitions to fill the space. The second part of the challenge is to find an elegant way to turn the corner. The original builder took a pass and ended the arcs before reaching the corner, leaving a flat section on either side.

The face molding runs vertically as well as horizontally, and is applied on top of a face frame that is fastened to the front of the carcase. Where the hori-

zontal and vertical components of the moldings meet, the end of one part is coped to the other. At the top of the upper cabinet, there is no horizontal molding, so the end of the vertical molding stops abruptly with a straight cut where it butts into the cornice.

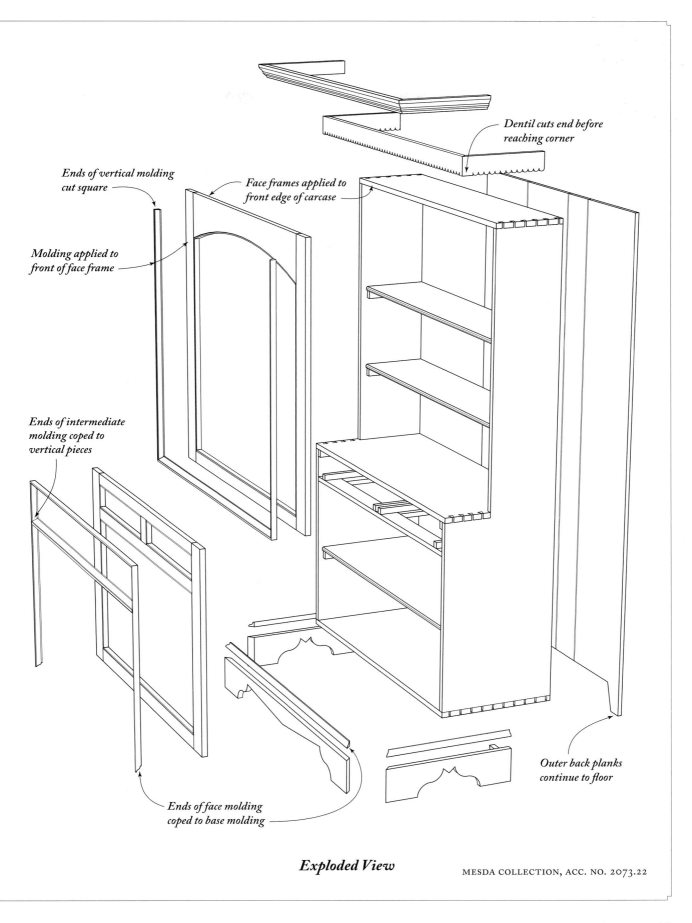

Dentil cuts end before reaching corner

Ends of vertical molding cut square

Face frames applied to front edge of carcase

Molding applied to front of face frame

Ends of intermediate molding coped to vertical pieces

Outer back planks continue to floor

Ends of face molding coped to base molding

**Exploded View**

MESDA COLLECTION, ACC. NO. 2073.22

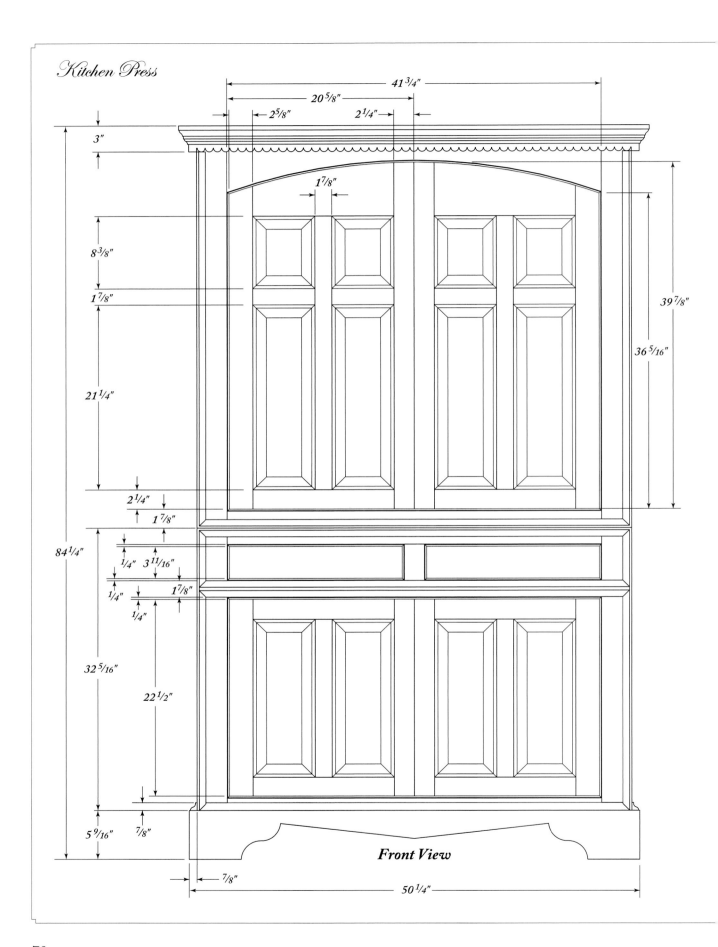

Front View

Kitchen Press

41 3/4"
20 5/8"
2 5/8"
2 1/4"
3"
1 7/8"
8 3/8"
1 7/8"
39 7/8"
36 5/16"
21 1/4"
2 1/4"
1 7/8"
84 1/4"
1/4"  3 11/16"
1/4"  1 7/8"
1/4"
32 5/16"
22 1/2"
5 9/16"  7/8"
7/8"
50 1/4"

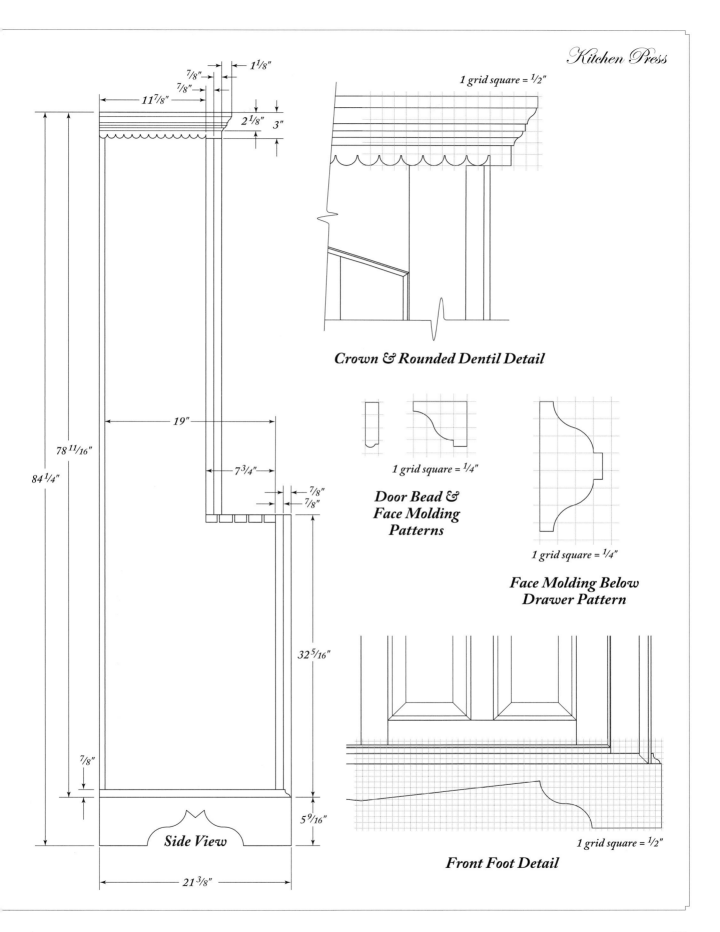

*1 grid square = 1/2"*

**Crown & Rounded Dentil Detail**

*1 grid square = 1/4"*

**Door Bead &
Face Molding
Patterns**

*1 grid square = 1/4"*

**Face Molding Below
Drawer Pattern**

11 7/8"

7/8"

7/8"

1 1/8"

2 1/8"    3"

19"

7 3/4"

7/8"
7/8"

78 11/16"

84 1/4"

32 5/16"

7/8"

5 9/16"

**Side View**

21 3/8"

*1 grid square = 1/2"*

**Front Foot Detail**

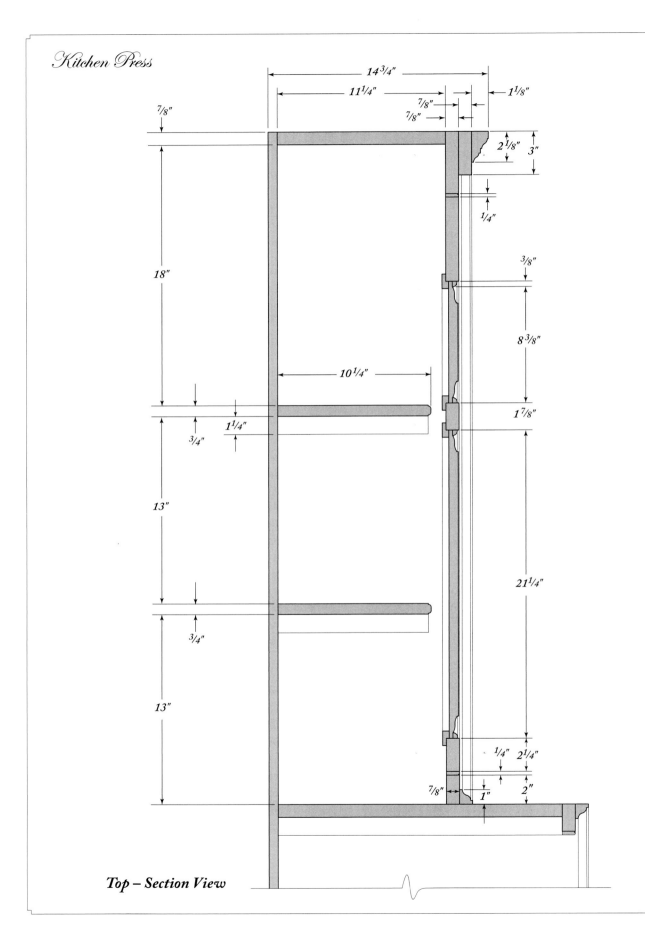

Kitchen Press

14³/₄"

11¹/₄"

⁷/₈"

1¹/₈"

⁷/₈"

⁷/₈"

2¹/₈"

3"

¹/₄"

³/₈"

18"

8³/₈"

10¹/₄"

1¹/₄"

1⁷/₈"

³/₄"

13"

21¹/₄"

³/₄"

13"

¹/₄"

2¹/₄"

⁷/₈"

1"

2"

***Top – Section View***

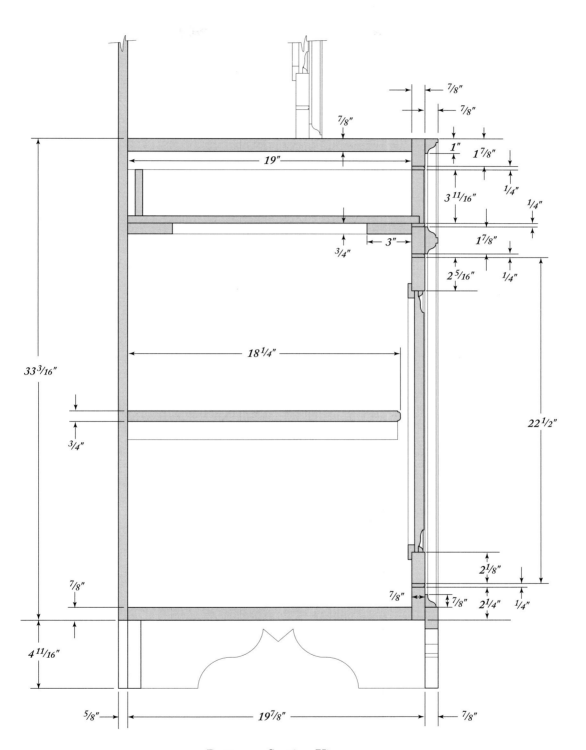

**Bottom – Section View**

# Nine-drawer Chest

*Built 1780–1790
in the Piedmont Region of North Carolina
of walnut, poplar & oak*

In the Northeast, ornate forms of furniture were favored, but in much of the South, the preference was for "furniture in the neat and plain style." Neat and plain also became the preferred style in England at the time, a refinement that called for simpler shapes and pleasing proportions.

The feet on this chest are an example of this unadorned approach. The overall shape and proportions are similar to fancier pieces, but the show faces are all within the same plane rather than worked to an ogee shape. The base and cornice moldings are also kept simple, with gentle curves and rounded edges and fewer steps within each molding profile.

## Proportions in Perspective

The graduation and arrangement of the drawers is pleasing to the eye, but does not seem to follow any imposed mathematical system. The original builder was likely unaware of the Golden Mean or the Fibonacci Sequence and instead chose to be guided by his own eye, judgement and experience.

Construction is solid, simple and straightforward, with a dovetailed case and a simple system of supporting and guiding the drawers. The escutcheons at the top of the drawers are inlays of a light color to contrast to the walnut primary wood. The drawer boxes of the original were poplar, and the drawer runners were oak.

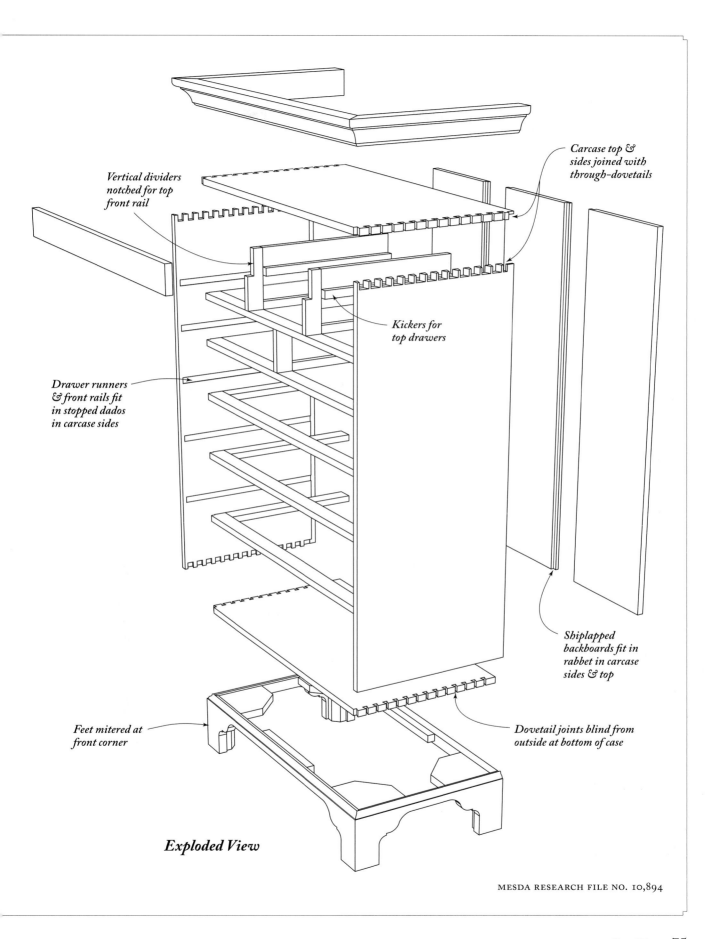

Carcase top &
sides joined with
through-dovetails

Vertical dividers
notched for top
front rail

Kickers for
top drawers

Drawer runners
& front rails fit
in stopped dados
in carcase sides

Shiplapped
backboards fit in
rabbet in carcase
sides & top

Feet mitered at
front corner

Dovetail joints blind from
outside at bottom of case

**Exploded View**

MESDA RESEARCH FILE NO. 10,894

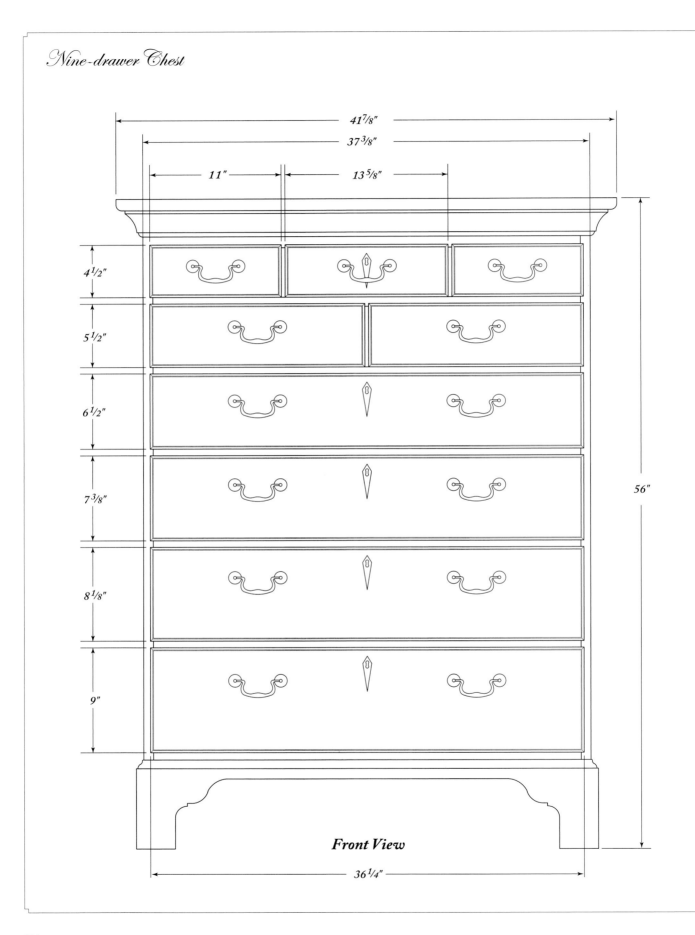

**Front View**

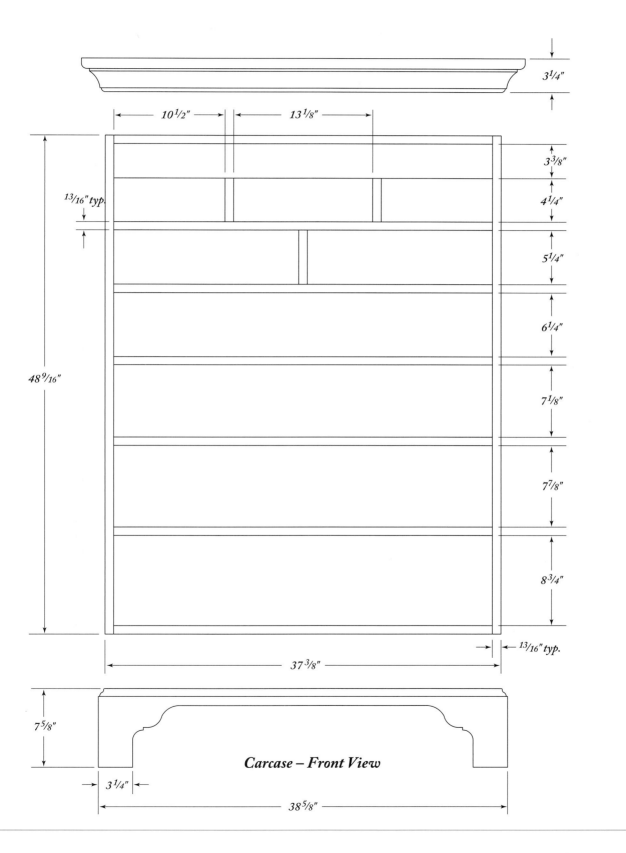

3¹/₄"

10¹/₂"    13¹/₈"

3³/₈"

4¹/₄"

¹³/₁₆" typ.

5¹/₄"

48⁹/₁₆"

6¹/₄"

7¹/₈"

7⁷/₈"

8³/₄"

¹³/₁₆" typ.

37³/₈"

7⁵/₈"

**Carcase – Front View**

3¹/₄"

38⁵/₈"

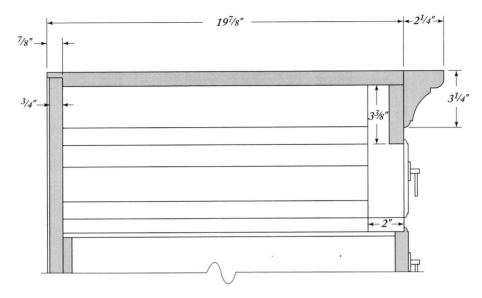

**Section View at Top**

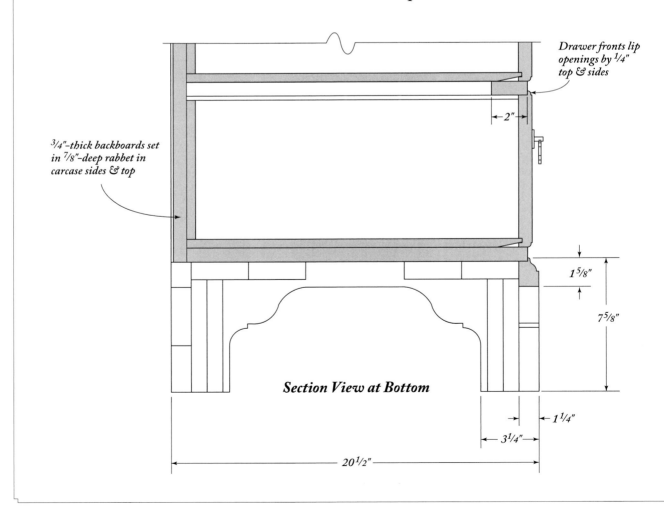

³/₄"-thick backboards set
in ⁷/₈"-deep rabbet in
carcase sides & top

Drawer fronts lip
openings by ¹/₄"
top & sides

**Section View at Bottom**

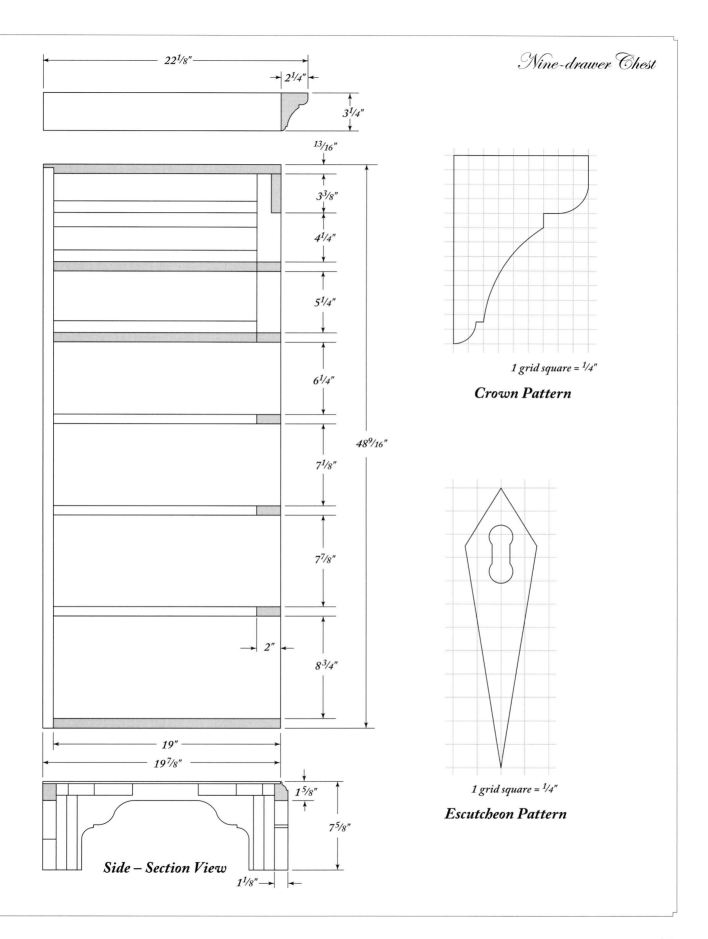

22<sup>1</sup>/8"

2<sup>1</sup>/4"

3<sup>1</sup>/4"

13/16"

3<sup>3</sup>/8"

4<sup>1</sup>/4"

5<sup>1</sup>/4"

6<sup>1</sup>/4"

48<sup>9</sup>/16"

7<sup>1</sup>/8"

*1 grid square = <sup>1</sup>/4"*

**Crown Pattern**

7<sup>7</sup>/8"

2"

8<sup>3</sup>/4"

19"

19<sup>7</sup>/8"

1<sup>5</sup>/8"

7<sup>5</sup>/8"

**Side – Section View**

1<sup>1</sup>/8"

*1 grid square = <sup>1</sup>/4"*

**Escutcheon Pattern**

# Five-drawer Chest

*Built circa 1840
in the Piedmont Region of North Carolina
of walnut & yellow pine*

One of the latest pieces of furniture in this book, this five-drawer chest has simple yet elegant details. No joinery is visible from the outside of the case and the moldings are small in scale and simple in profile. This minimalist approach relies on overall proportions for its pleasing appearance. The case is nearly a square, and those who believe in graduating drawers by formula will struggle to find one to apply to this chest.

The simplified and stylized cabriole legs terminate in trifid feet at the front. The back legs have an entirely different profile, tapering from front to back. It is impossible to say if this was done for style or for economy. The legs are connected with scrolled rails that alternate arches with short, straight sections on the front that widen at the ends.

There isn't much surface area where the carcase sits on the rails of the base, and it would be reasonable to assume the presence of glue blocks between the long rails and the case bottom. These would be a prudent addition. This piece is in a private collection, so the internal construction details represent a "best-case" scenario. There is a good chance that instead of the web frames shown, the drawer supports were simply attached to the sides of the case.

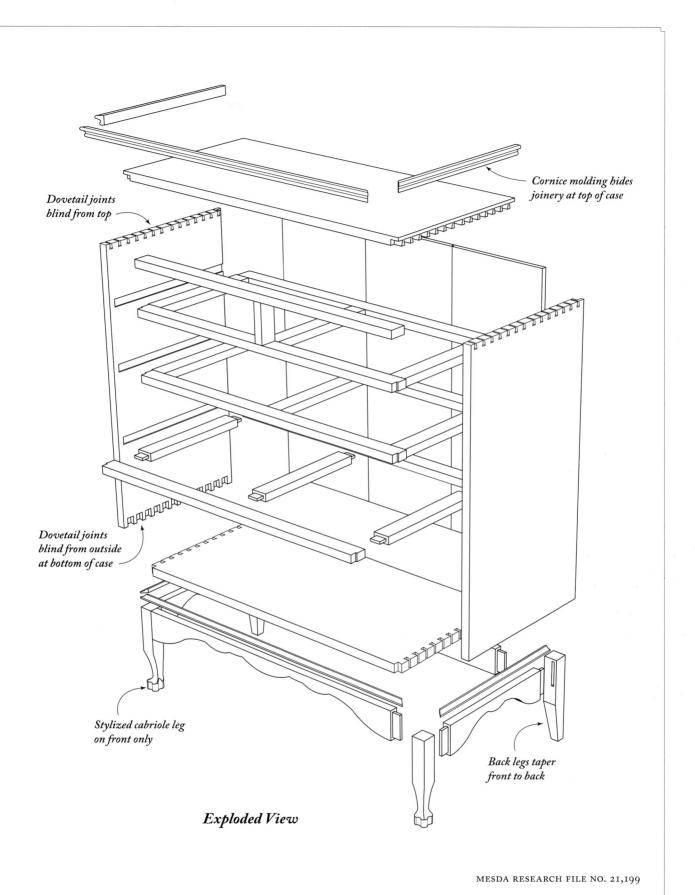

Cornice molding hides
joinery at top of case

Dovetail joints
blind from top

Dovetail joints
blind from outside
at bottom of case

Stylized cabriole leg
on front only

Back legs taper
front to back

**Exploded View**

MESDA RESEARCH FILE NO. 21,199

*Five-drawer Chest*

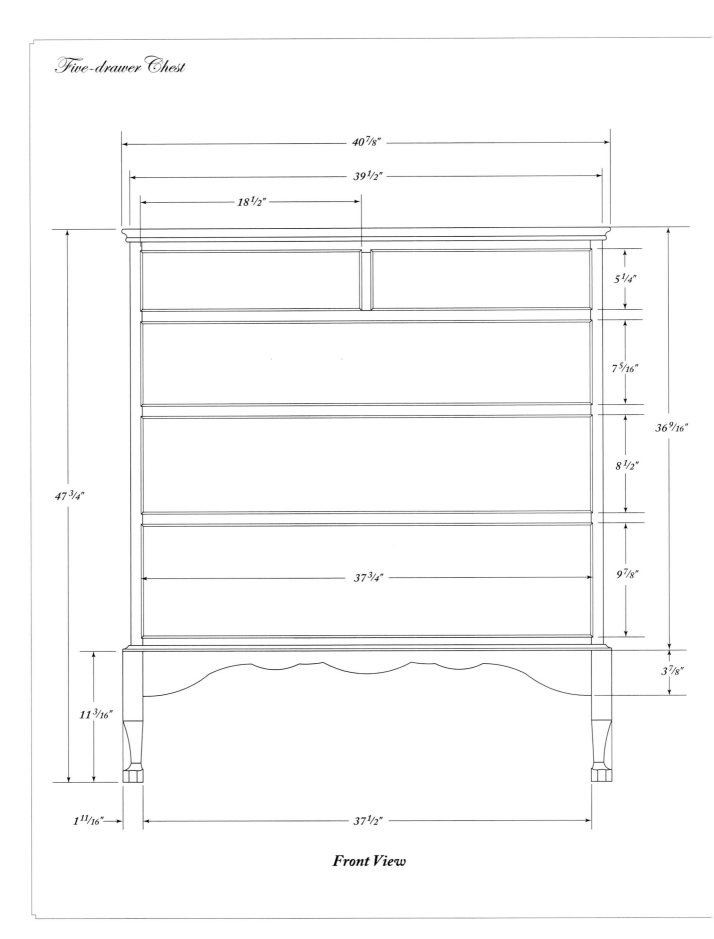

40⁷/₈″

39¹/₂″

18¹/₂″

5¹/₄″

7⁵/₁₆″

36⁹/₁₆″

8¹/₂″

47³/₄″

9⁷/₈″

37³/₄″

3⁷/₈″

11³/₁₆″

1¹¹/₁₆″

37¹/₂″

**Front View**

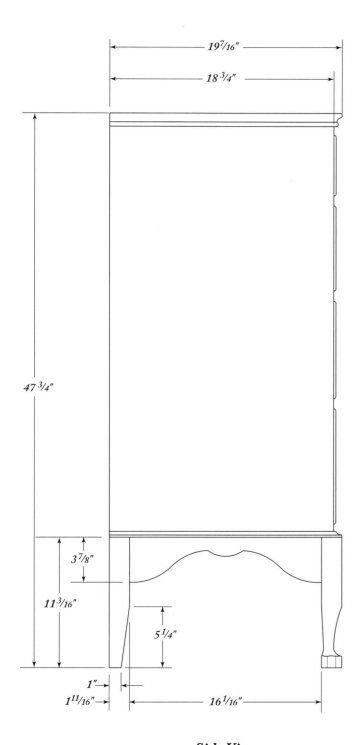

19 7/16"

18 3/4"

47 3/4"

3 7/8"

11 3/16"

5 1/4"

1"

1 11/16"

16 1/16"

**Side View**

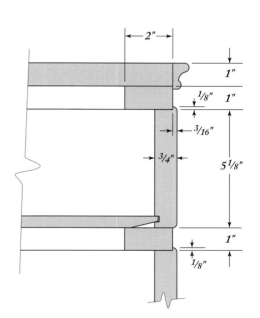

2"

1"

1/8" 1"

3/16"

3/4"

5 1/8"

1"

1/8"

**Section at Top Drawer**

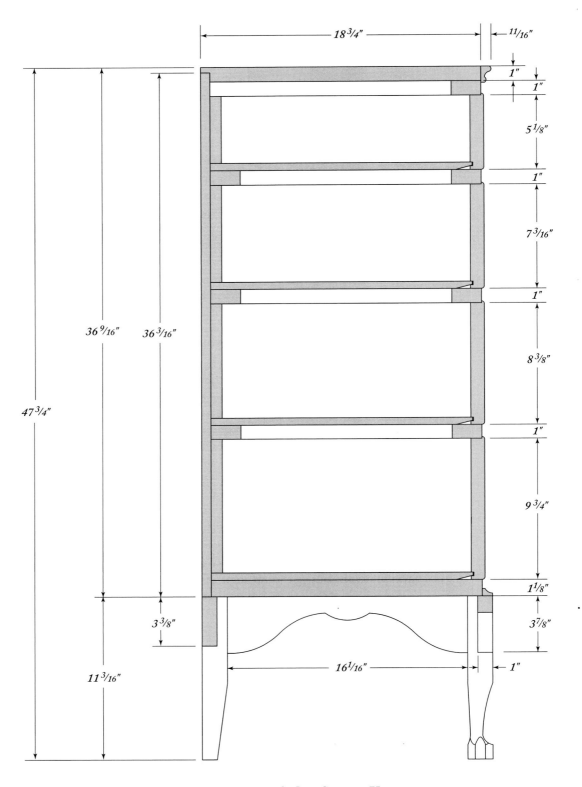

18³/₄"

11/₁₆"

1"

1"

5¹/₈"

1"

7³/₁₆"

1"

8³/₈"

1"

9³/₄"

1¹/₈"

3⁷/₈"

1"

16¹/₁₆"

36⁹/₁₆"

36³/₁₆"

47³/₄"

3³/₈"

11³/₁₆"

**Side – Section View**

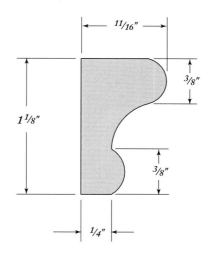

**Cornice Molding Profile**

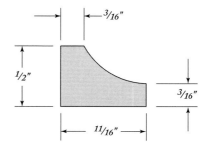

**Transition Molding Profile**

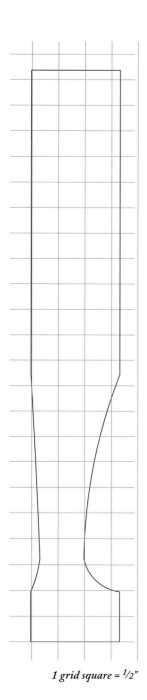

*1 grid square = ¹/₂"*

**Front Leg Pattern**

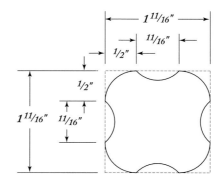

**Carved Foot Profile**

# Miniature Chest

*Built 1780–1790*
*most likely in the Piedmont Region of North Carolina*
*of walnut & yellow pine*

mall chests with locking drawers were used to securely store valuable items, perhaps jewelry, spices or medicines. From our modern viewpoint it is easy to be cynical and question the logic. A thief could easily carry away the entire case if he wanted all of what was within. The aim was not, however, to stop an intruder, but to prevent members of the household from helping themselves to an undue or disallowed portion of the contents.

For today's woodworker, a small case of this form is an excellent introduction to and means of practicing the joinery and details found in a larger piece of furniture. In this example, the typical molding around the sides and front of the top is not used. Instead, the top overhangs, creating a visual break and a shadow line.

This is also an example of how the original makers viewed the use of dovetails. The current trend is to show off the joinery as a testament to the maker's skills. In the 18th century, however, dovetails were used because of their utility and would often be hidden behind a molding, as at the bottom of this piece, or visible only from one side, as in the bracket feet. The goal was to make a piece that was attractive overall, and would stay together for hundreds of years.

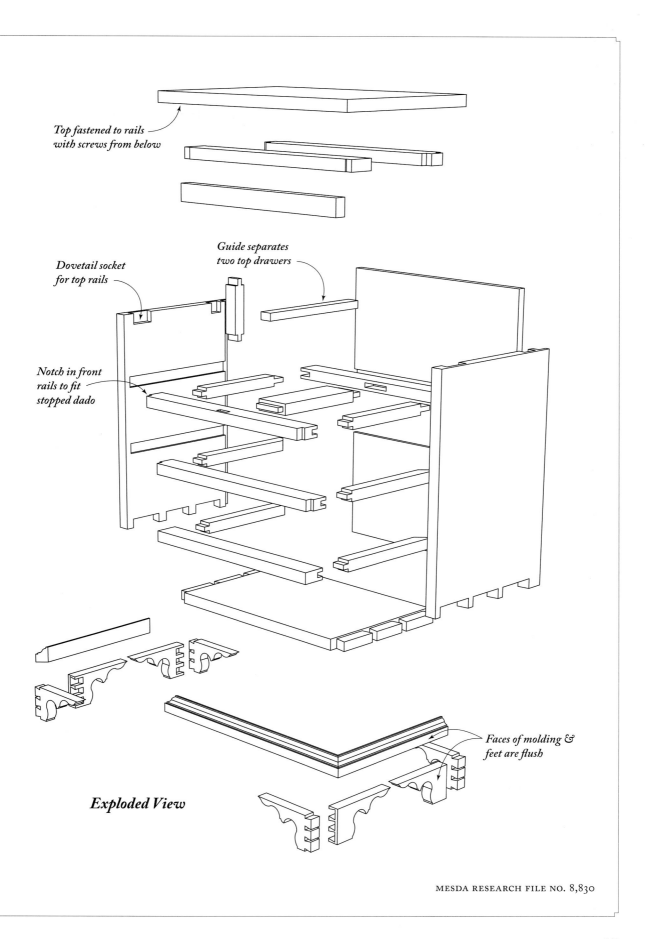

Top fastened to rails
with screws from below

Guide separates
two top drawers

Dovetail socket
for top rails

Notch in front
rails to fit
stopped dado

Faces of molding &
feet are flush

**Exploded View**

MESDA RESEARCH FILE NO. 8,830

## Miniature Chest

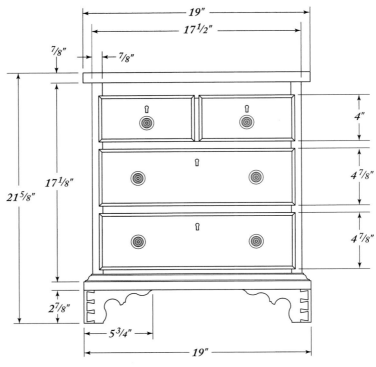

19"

17¹/₂"

7/8"

7/8"

4"

17¹/₈"

4⁷/₈"

21⁵/₈"

4⁷/₈"

2⁷/₈"

5³/₄"

19"

**Front View**

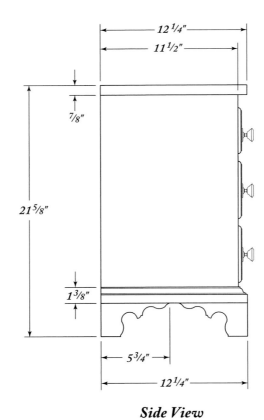

12¹/₄"

11¹/₂"

7/8"

21⁵/₈"

1³/₈"

5³/₄"

12¹/₄"

**Side View**

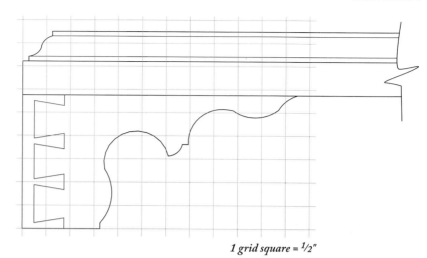

*1 grid square = 1/2"*

## Foot & Molding Detail Pattern

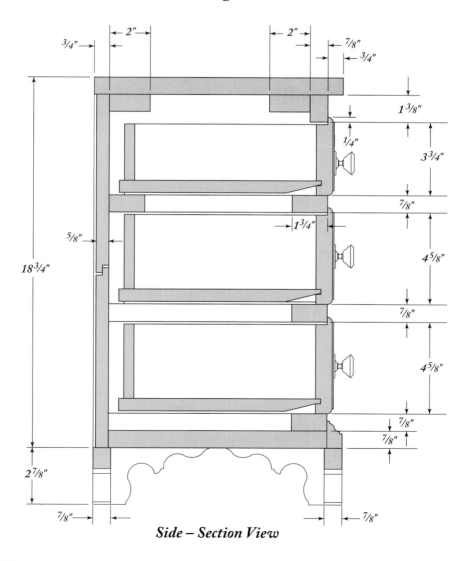

*Side – Section View*

# Cellarettes & Sideboards

∞

# Kentucky Chest

*Built circa 1800
in Kentucky
of cherry, walnut & poplar*

Kentucky furniture was often made of cherry and adorned with simple, elegant and lyrical inlays of lighter colored wood. In this sugar chest, the corner fans are sand shaded, and the lines in the bellflowers are incised and darkened. If your impression of Kentucky in 1800 is Daniel Boone in the wilderness, try to envision this piece in a log cabin; it obviously had a nicer home. After the Cumberland Gap was open, Kentucky quickly became a civilized and sophisticated place.

Small cases on stands carry a number of names, and served different purposes in different places. In much of the South, these pieces were indeed for the storage of sugar, an essential and expensive commodity. In other areas, especially the East, the small box on stand was intended for storing liquor.

Construction of this case is straightforward; it is a dovetailed box on a stand. The most challenging part of building a reproduction of this chest might well be finding suitable material. A 20"-wide board without sapwood was likely common at the time, but today it would require a diligent hunt to find. Another clue about the abundance of hardwood in the period is the use of walnut for the drawer guides, while poplar was used elsewhere in the original as a secondary wood.

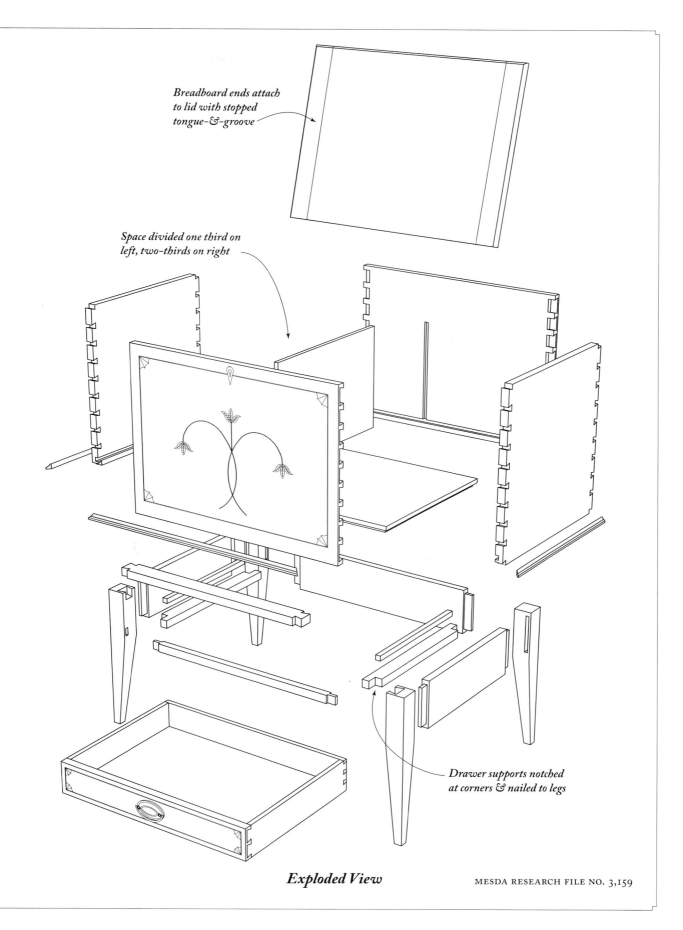

*Breadboard ends attach to lid with stopped tongue-&-groove*

*Space divided one third on left, two-thirds on right*

*Drawer supports notched at corners & nailed to legs*

**Exploded View**

MESDA RESEARCH FILE NO. 3,159

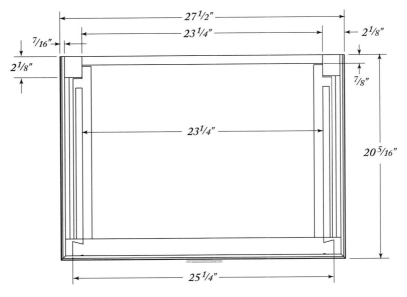

27¹/₂"
23¹/₄"
2¹/₈"
7/16"
2¹/₈"
7/8"
23¹/₄"
20⁵/₁₆"
25¹/₄"

**Base – Top View**

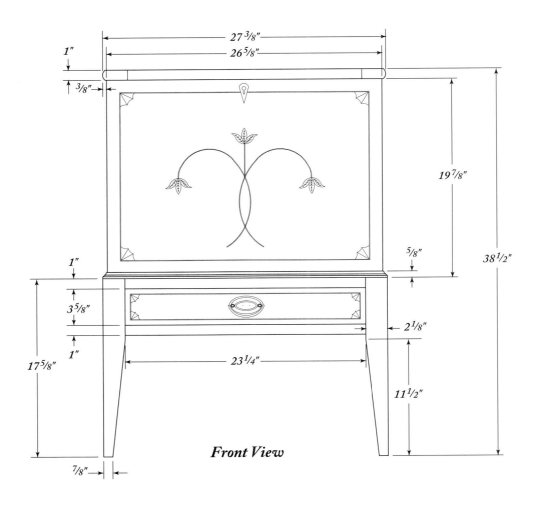

27³/₈"
26⁵/₈"
1"
3/8"
19⁷/₈"
5/8"
38¹/₂"
1"
3⁵/₈"
2¹/₈"
1"
23¹/₄"
17⁵/₈"
11¹/₂"
7/8"

**Front View**

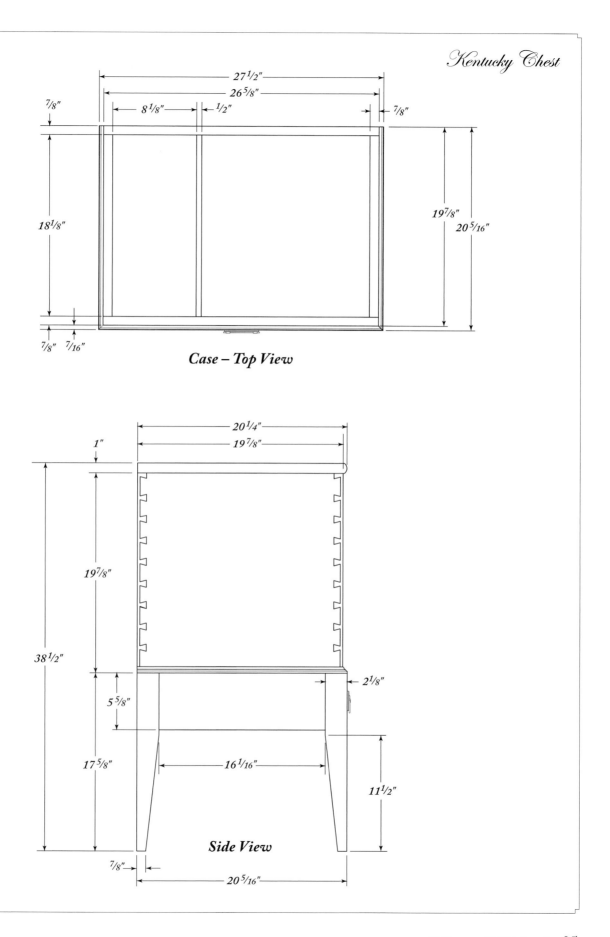

**Case – Top View**

**Side View**

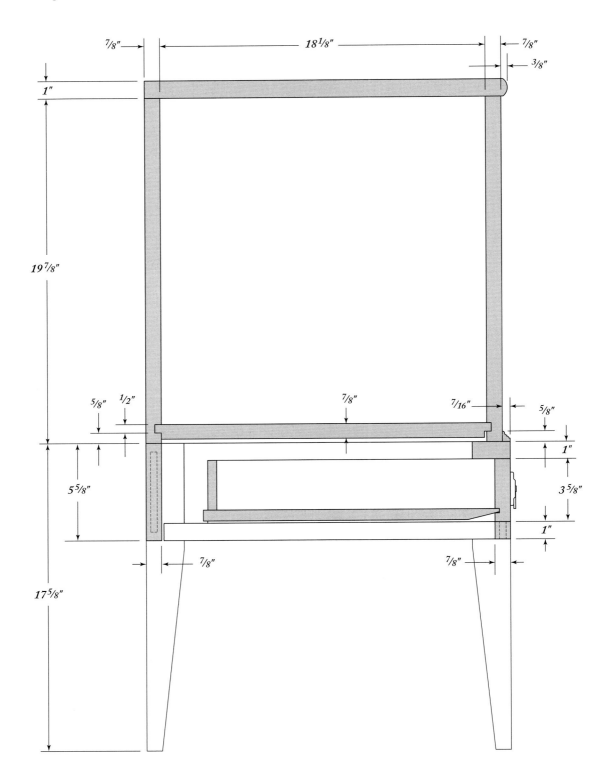

**Side – Section View**

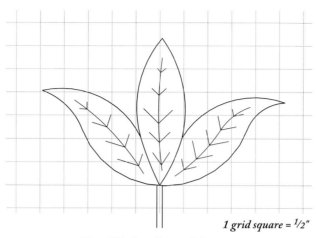

*1 grid square = $^1/2$"*

**Petal Inlay Detail Pattern**

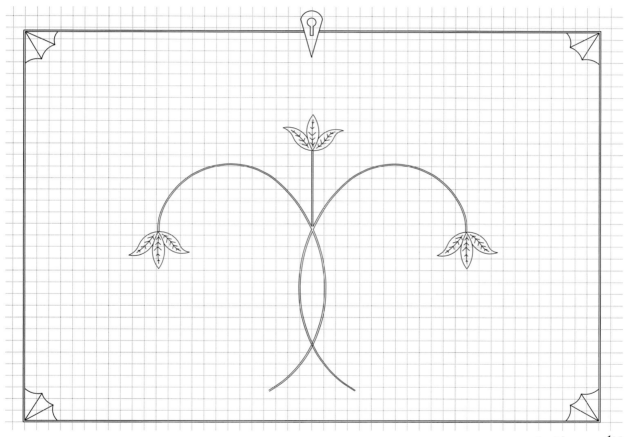

*1 grid square = $^1/2$"*

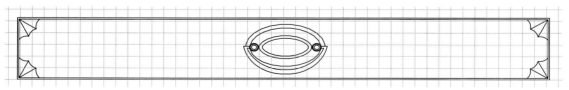

*1 grid square = $^1/2$"*

**Front Inlay Details & Patterns**

# Sideboard

❦

*Built 1795–1805*
*most likely in the Piedmont Region of South Carolina*
*of walnut, light & dark wood inlay & yellow pine*

imple forms don't mean crude construction or lack of sophistication. This is the type of piece that looks good from a distance and reveals nice details on closer examination. Instead of an applied molding, the edges of the top are worked to a simple cove and there is a gentle cove just above the lower edge of the backsplash. The band at the bottom of the rail below the drawers is a strip of darker wood bounded by two strips of light wood, and this inlay continues across the legs and returns on the sides.

The scalloped brackets between the lower case and the legs add a lighthearted design element while softening the transition. The small scratch bead around the drawer fronts sets them off while relating to the vertical stringing on the legs. The backsplash is an interesting yet subtle shape rising in a gentle curve from the rounded ends to the central peak. On the whole, this piece says, "welcome to our table," without being pretentious or overbearing.

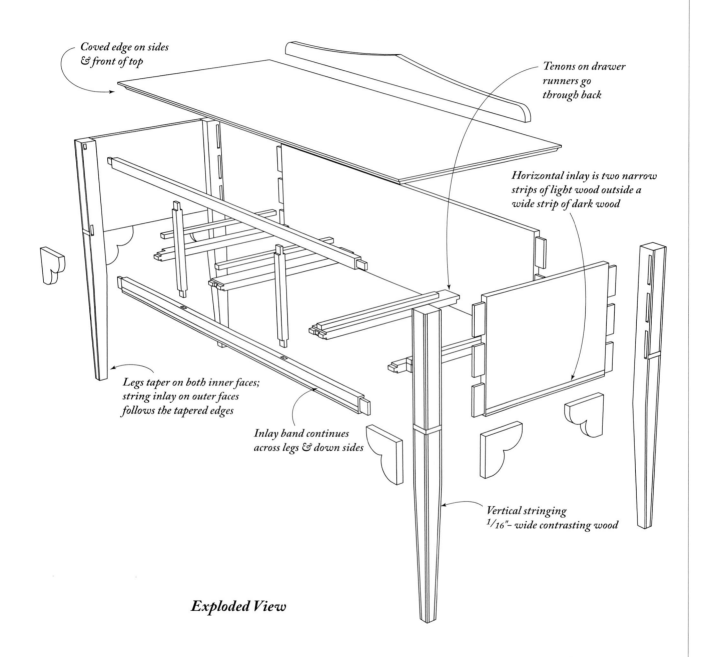

*Coved edge on sides & front of top*

*Tenons on drawer runners go through back*

*Horizontal inlay is two narrow strips of light wood outside a wide strip of dark wood*

*Legs taper on both inner faces; string inlay on outer faces follows the tapered edges*

*Inlay band continues across legs & down sides*

*Vertical stringing ¹⁄₁₆"- wide contrasting wood*

**Exploded View**

MESDA RESEARCH FILE NO. 10,898

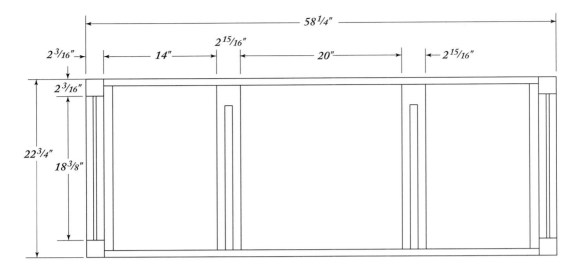

**Top View – Top & Drawers Removed**

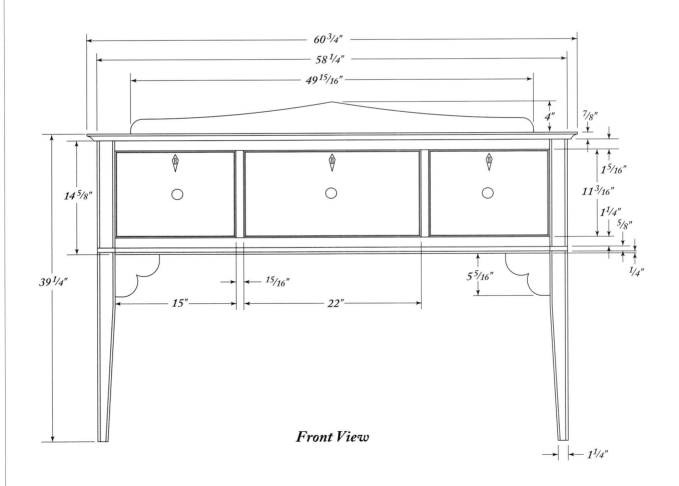

**Front View**

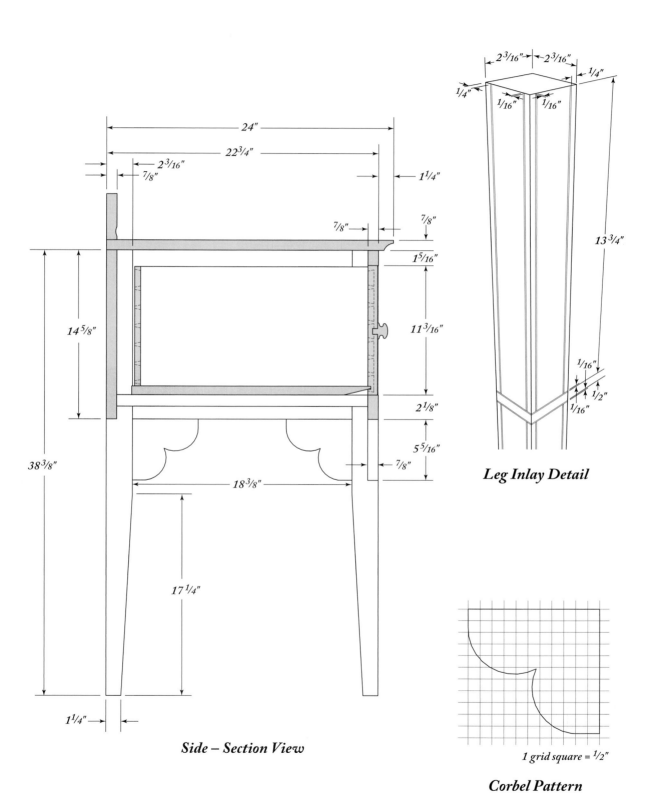

2³/₁₆" — 2³/₁₆"

1/4"

1/4"

1/16" 1/16"

13³/4"

1/16"

1/2"

1/16"

**Leg Inlay Detail**

24"

22³/4"

2³/₁₆"

7/8"

1¹/4"

7/8"

7/8"

1⁵/₁₆"

11³/₁₆"

14⁵/8"

2¹/8"

5⁵/₁₆"

7/8"

38³/8"

18³/8"

17¹/4"

1¹/4"

**Side – Section View**

*1 grid square = ¹/₂"*

**Corbel Pattern**

# Cellarette

*Built circa 1810
most likely in the Piedmont Region
of North Carolina
of walnut & yellow pine*

Some would argue that this piece should rightly be called a sugar chest rather than a cellarette. The term "cellarette" is a more modern invention. In the period, cases of this form would have been called a "liquor box" or "gin box." The difference between the two is generally determined by how the inner case is divided. Sugar chests usually had a large division for loose white sugar and a smaller division for stacking blocks of brown sugar. In this piece, the drawer is also divided, into four equal sections.

The moldings on this piece serve a practical as well as a decorative purpose. On the lid, the molding is wider than the lid is thick, hanging down to retard the infiltration of sultry southern air to the contents inside. At the top of the base, the molding sticks up to prevent the upper case from sliding off the stand. The upper case can be removed, allowing it to be carried separately when the contents, either liquid or solid, need to be replenished.

As can be seen in the photo, nails were used extensively for attaching the applied moldings to the lid and base. It was also common at the time to attach the bottom of the case with nails, instead of fitting it into a groove as we would be apt to do today.

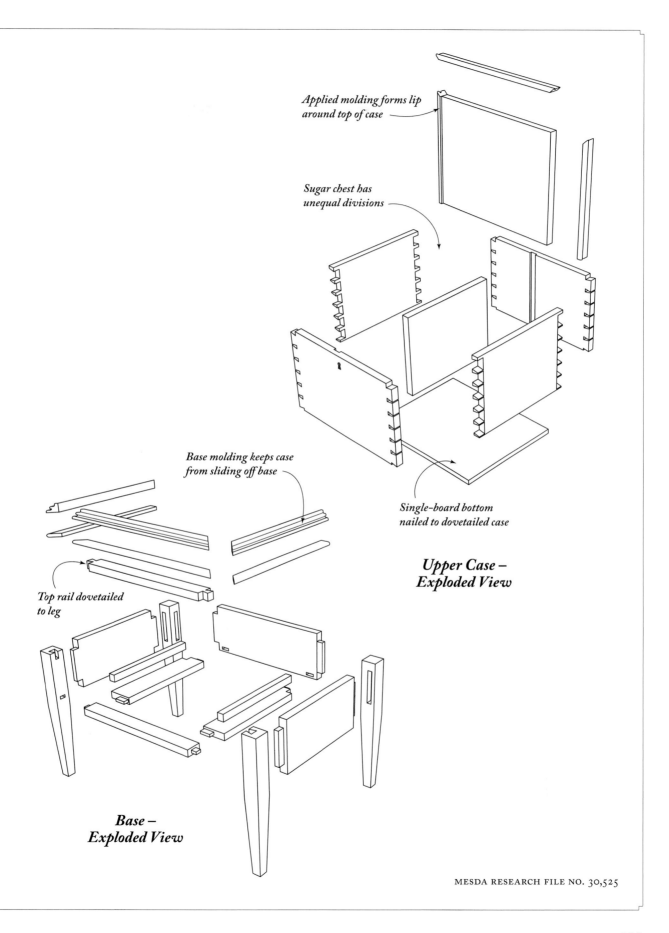

Applied molding forms lip
around top of case

Sugar chest has
unequal divisions

Base molding keeps case
from sliding off base

Single–board bottom
nailed to dovetailed case

*Upper Case –*
*Exploded View*

Top rail dovetailed
to leg

*Base –*
*Exploded View*

MESDA RESEARCH FILE NO. 30,525

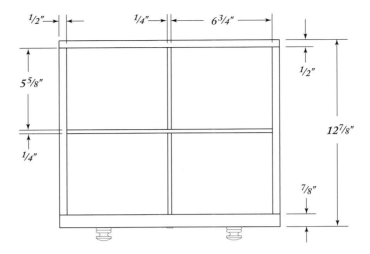

**Drawer – Top View**

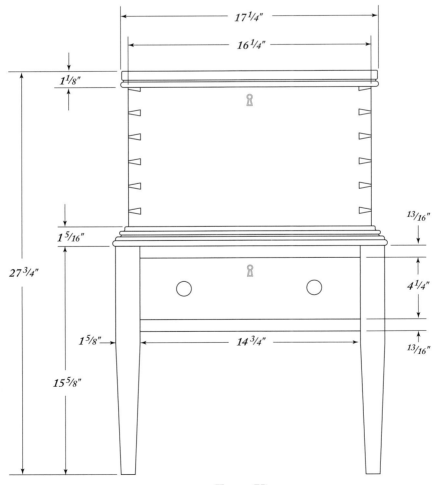

**Front View**

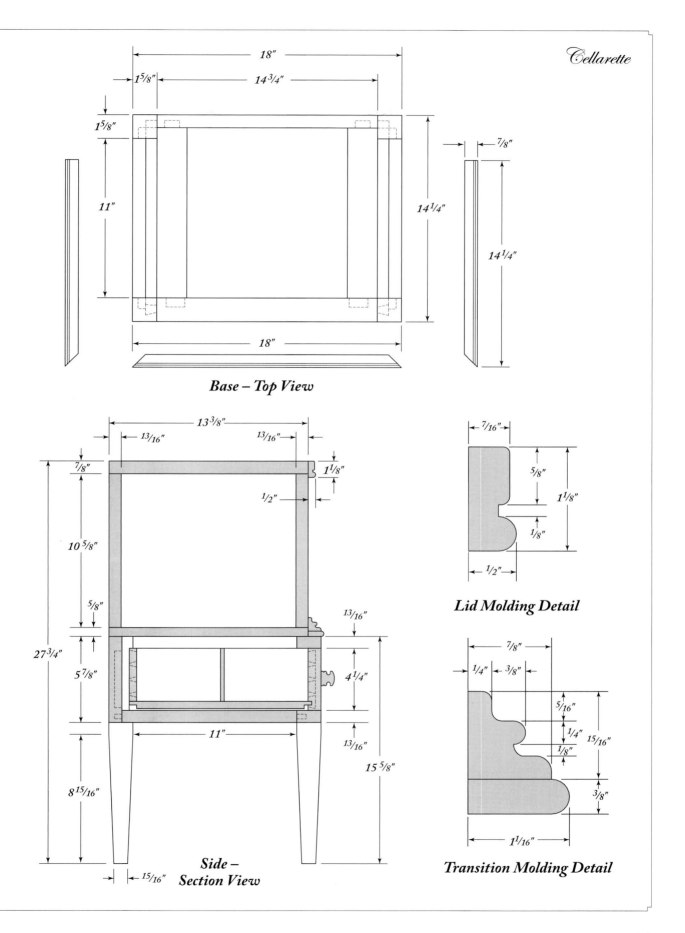

**Base – Top View**

18"
1⁵/₈"
14³/₄"
1⁵/₈"
11"
14¹/₄"
18"
⁷/₈"
14¹/₄"

**Lid Molding Detail**

⁷/₁₆"
5/8"
1¹/₈"
¹/₈"
¹/₂"

**Side – Section View**

13³/₈"
¹³/₁₆"
¹³/₁₆"
⁷/₈"
1¹/₈"
¹/₂"
10⁵/₈"
5/8"
27³/₄"
5⁷/₈"
13/₁₆"
4¹/₄"
11"
13/₁₆"
15⁵/₈"
8¹⁵/₁₆"
¹⁵/₁₆"

**Transition Molding Detail**

⁷/₈"
¹/₄"
³/₈"
⁵/₁₆"
¹/₄"
15/₁₆"
¹/₈"
³/₈"
1¹/₁₆"

# Five-drawer Sideboard

༄

*Built 1785-1795*
*most likely in the Piedmont Region of South Carolina*
*of walnut & yellow pine*

Cabinetmakers in different eras have different attitudes about methods of joinery and the use of fasteners. This sideboard is a good case with which to study the differences between then and now. Today, nails are frowned on for finished surfaces, but in this sideboard, the molding around the top and the brackets on the legs are nailed in place. Nails were also acceptable as structural fasteners; in the case interior, the drawer runners are toenailed into the front rail.

Other parts of the interior are joined with through-mortise-and-tenon joints. In today's world, through-mortises-and-tenons are similar to dovetails – the attitude is, if you go to the trouble to make such a joint, it should be in a location where you can show it off. Two hundred years ago in South Carolina, sound construction trumped a cabinetmaker's ego, and running the tenons all the way through in an unseen location meant maximum strength for an otherwise short tenon.

The cockbeading around the perimeter of the drawer fronts is also applied; it is mitered at the corners and nailed in place. The question of how to attach the top (a source of debate about methodology

and wood movement today) was answered by driving wooden pegs through the top and into the rails. Today's "Rules for Furniture Construction" prohibit methods that have worked well, at least with this piece, for more than 200 years.

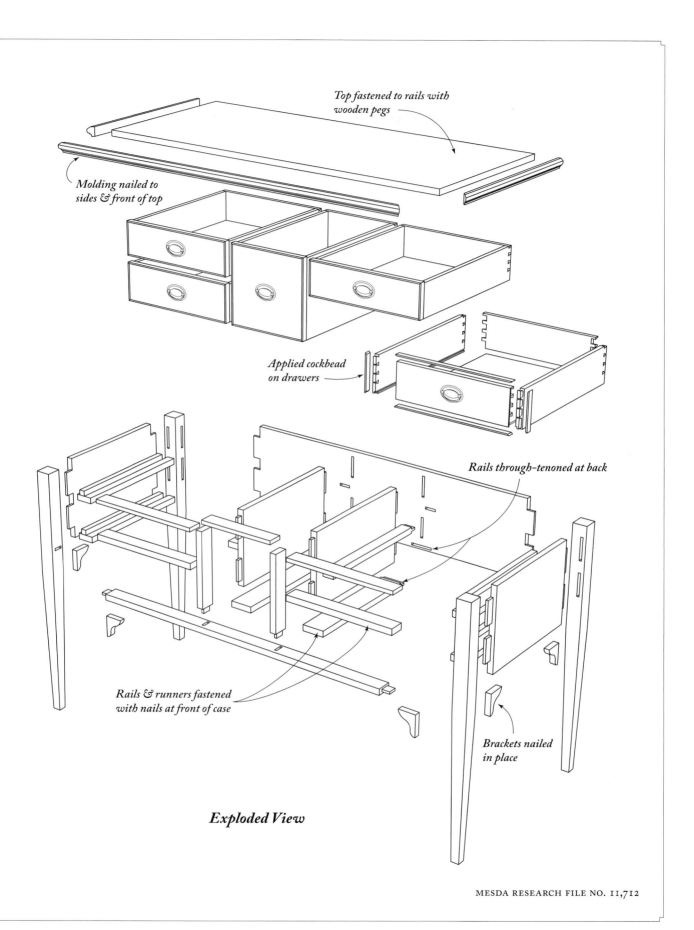

Top fastened to rails with wooden pegs

Molding nailed to sides & front of top

Applied cockbead on drawers

Rails through-tenoned at back

Rails & runners fastened with nails at front of case

Brackets nailed in place

**Exploded View**

MESDA RESEARCH FILE NO. 11,712

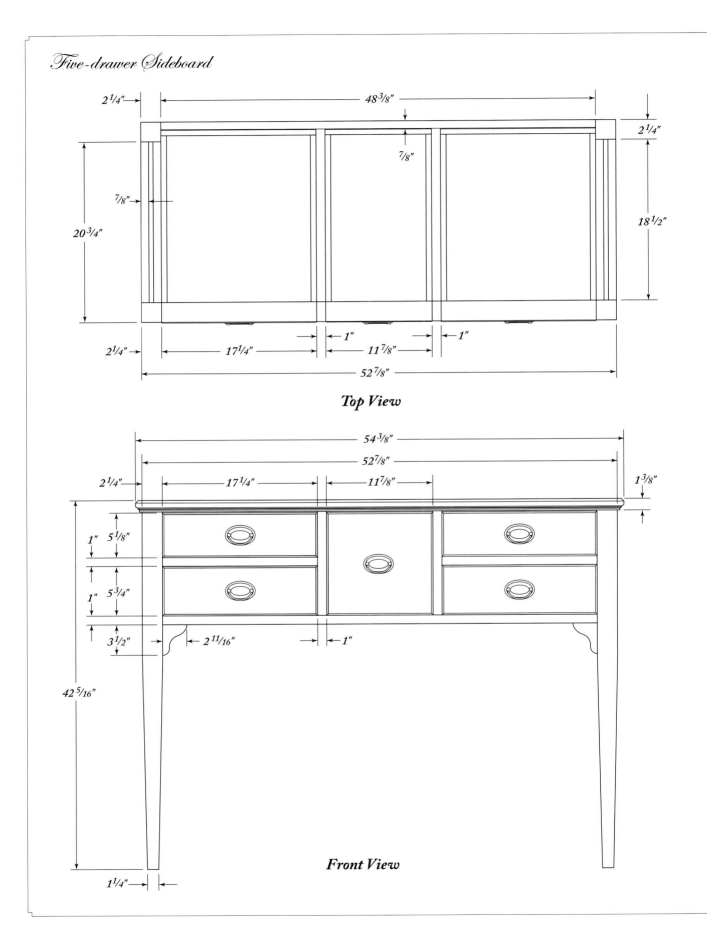

*Five-drawer Sideboard*

2 1/4"  48 3/8"  2 1/4"

7/8"

7/8"  18 1/2"

20 3/4"

1"  1"

2 1/4"  17 1/4"  11 7/8"

52 7/8"

**Top View**

54 3/8"

52 7/8"

2 1/4"  17 1/4"  11 7/8"  1 3/8"

1"  5 1/8"

1"  5 3/4"

3 1/2"  2 11/16"  1"

42 5/16"

1 1/4"

**Front View**

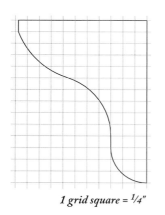

1 grid square = ¹/₄"

**Molding Pattern**

1 grid square = ¹/₄"

**Bracket Pattern**

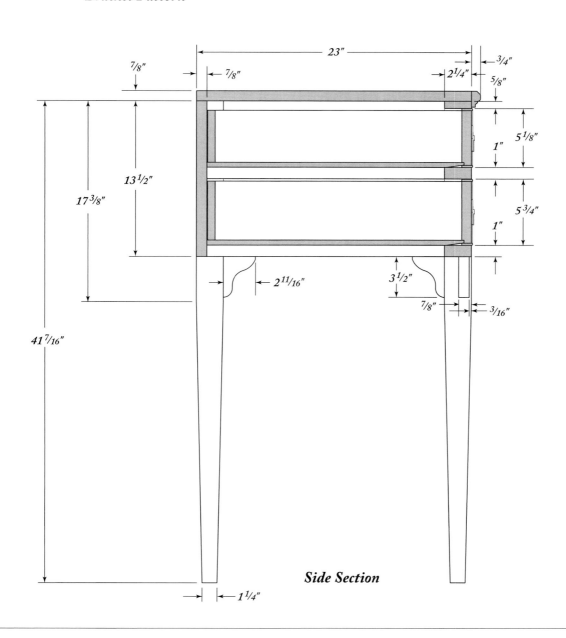

**Side Section**

# Sugar Chest

*Built 1840–1860
in Northeast Georgia
of yellow pine, painted*

The sugar chest is common in the South, but rarely seen north of the Mason-Dixon line. These chests provided protection from humidity and from members of the household who might be tempted to help themselves to this staple that was expensive at the time. A typical sugar chest had a divided interior, with one-third of the area reserved for stacking blocks of brown sugar, and two-thirds of the available space for loose white sugar.

This example has a third area for storage; there is a small till at the top of the larger section, divided into three small sections. This extra area may have been for the safekeeping of medicines or herbs. The construction of the till and the molding around the top reveal some quirks of the builder. The rest of the construction is simple and straightforward, but in these two areas the builder had to do some extra work in response to his own methods in other portions of the piece.

## Self-induced Complications

The simple molding runs around three sides of the lid. Across the front, the molding is nailed directly to the single wide board of the hinged lid. The ends of the lid are breadboard ends; cross-grain bands connected to the lid with a tongue-and-groove, and likely a couple of mortise-and-tenon joints. The molding returns are separate pieces; they are mitered at the front and terminate at the back.

Inside the chest, the panels have a raised field to fit within grooves in the legs and the rails. The main vertical divider fits in grooves that have been worked across the horizontal rails and the panels.

The small till also rests in stopped grooves that pass through the top rail and end within the panels, just past the ends of the raised panel field. Where the panels slope at their perimeters, the bottom must extend past the dividers to prevent the contents of the till from leaking into the lower section of the chest. One edge and one end of the nailed-on till bottom have been scribed to match the shape of these voids.

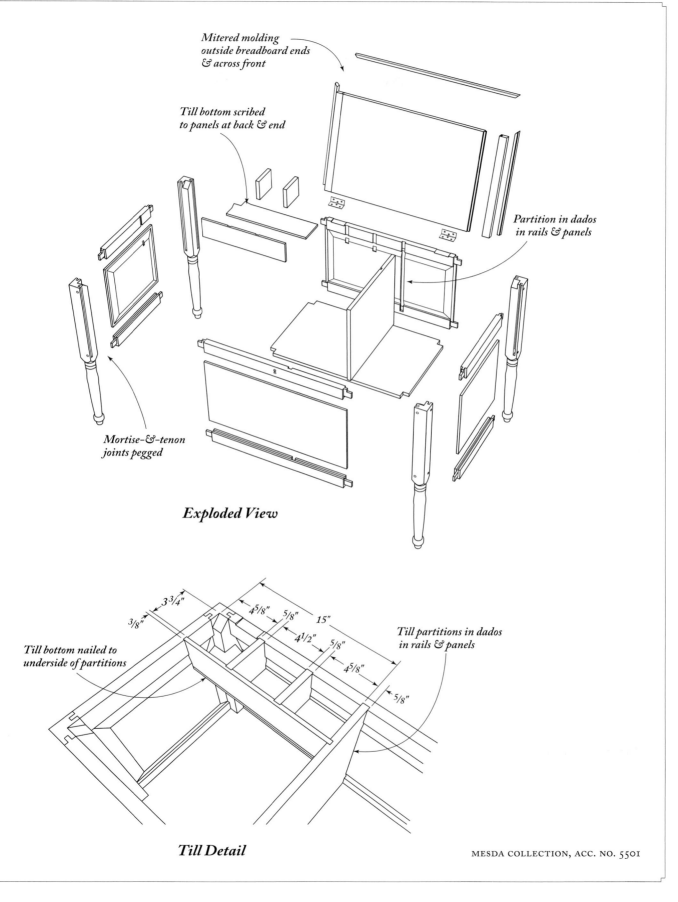

Mitered molding
outside breadboard ends
& across front

Till bottom scribed
to panels at back & end

Partition in dados
in rails & panels

Mortise-&-tenon
joints pegged

**Exploded View**

Till bottom nailed to
underside of partitions

3/8"

3 3/4"

4 5/8"

5/8"

15"

4 1/2"

5/8"

4 5/8"

5/8"

Till partitions in dados
in rails & panels

**Till Detail**

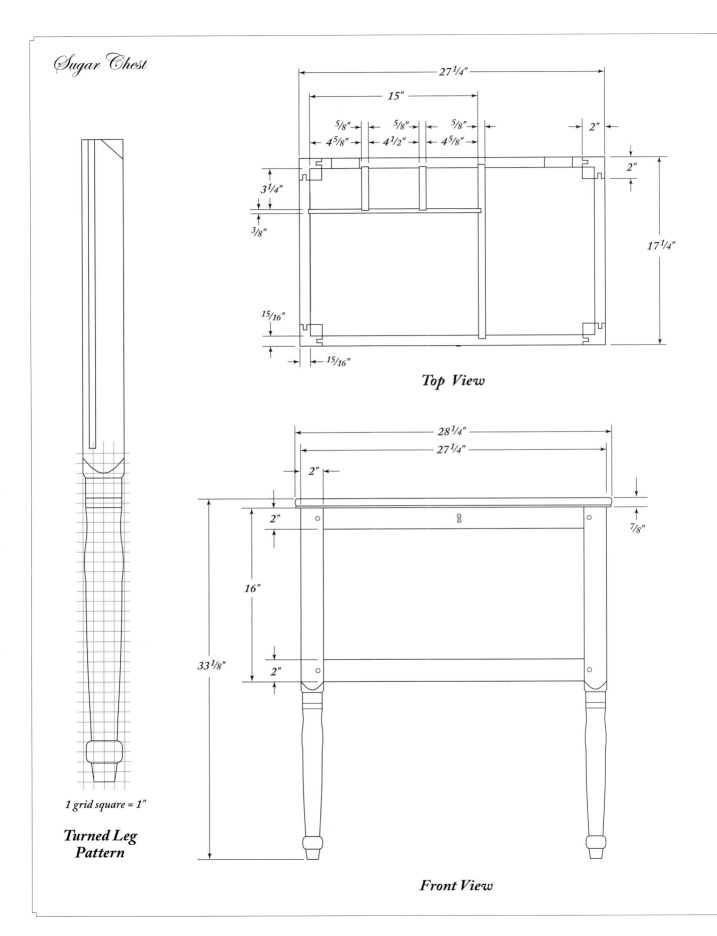

*Sugar Chest*

27¹/₄"

15"

⁵/₈"    ⁵/₈"    ⁵/₈"    2"

4⁵/₈"    4¹/₂"    4⁵/₈"

2"

3¹/₄"

2"

3/₈"

17¹/₄"

¹⁵/₁₆"

¹⁵/₁₆"

**Top View**

28¹/₄"

27¹/₄"

2"

2"

7/₈"

16"

33¹/₈"

2"

*1 grid square = 1"*

**Turned Leg
Pattern**

**Front View**

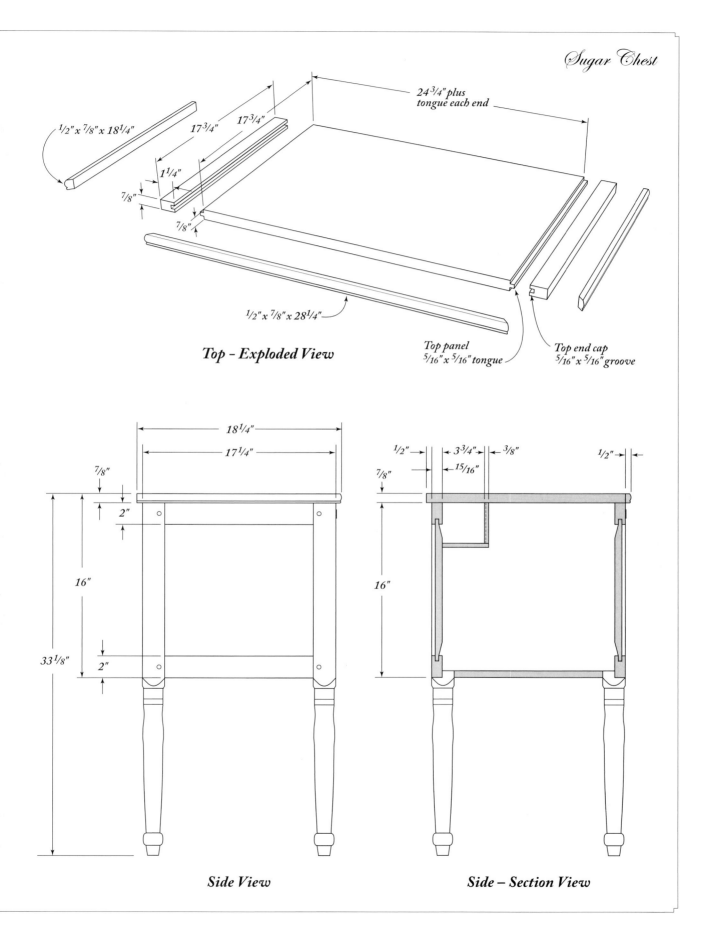

**Top - Exploded View**

$^1/_2"$ x $^7/_8"$ x $18^1/_4"$

$17^3/_4"$   $17^3/_4"$

$24^3/_4"$ plus tongue each end

$1^1/_4"$

$^7/_8"$

$^7/_8"$

$^1/_2"$ x $^7/_8"$ x $28^1/_4"$

Top panel $^5/_{16}"$ x $^5/_{16}"$ tongue

Top end cap $^5/_{16}"$ x $^5/_{16}"$ groove

$18^1/_4"$

$17^1/_4"$

$^7/_8"$

2"

16"

2"

$33^1/_8"$

**Side View**

$^1/_2"$   $3^3/_4"$   $^3/_8"$   $^1/_2"$

$^7/_8"$   $^{15}/_{16}"$

16"

**Side – Section View**

# Beds,
# Blanket Chests
# &
# Lady's Desk

# High-post Bedstead

*Built 1800–1820
in Southwest Virginia
of poplar*

**B**ed sizes were not standardized until recently, so reproducing this bed will require the builder to adjust the width and length to fit the size of a modern mattress. In the original, a secondary rail was placed inside the outer rails. On top of the inner rail were pegs; rope was woven around the pegs to support the mattress.

We left the pegs out of our drawings, reasoning that most readers would want to use modern bedding. The head and foot board are assembled as units; the long rails connecting them are removable. Tenons on the ends of the long rails fit mortises in the legs, and these joints are secured with bed bolts.

The corners of the upper frame are lap joints with a hole in the center of the joint. The finials at the top are loose, passing through the hole in the lap joint and into a hole in the top of the bedpost. This is one of the few pieces in this book to use poplar as a primary wood, but poplar was often used in some areas, particularly where immigrants from Germany settled. Poplar is a bit softer and easier to work than other hardwoods, and its working properties are similar to that of linden, a common wood used in Germany.

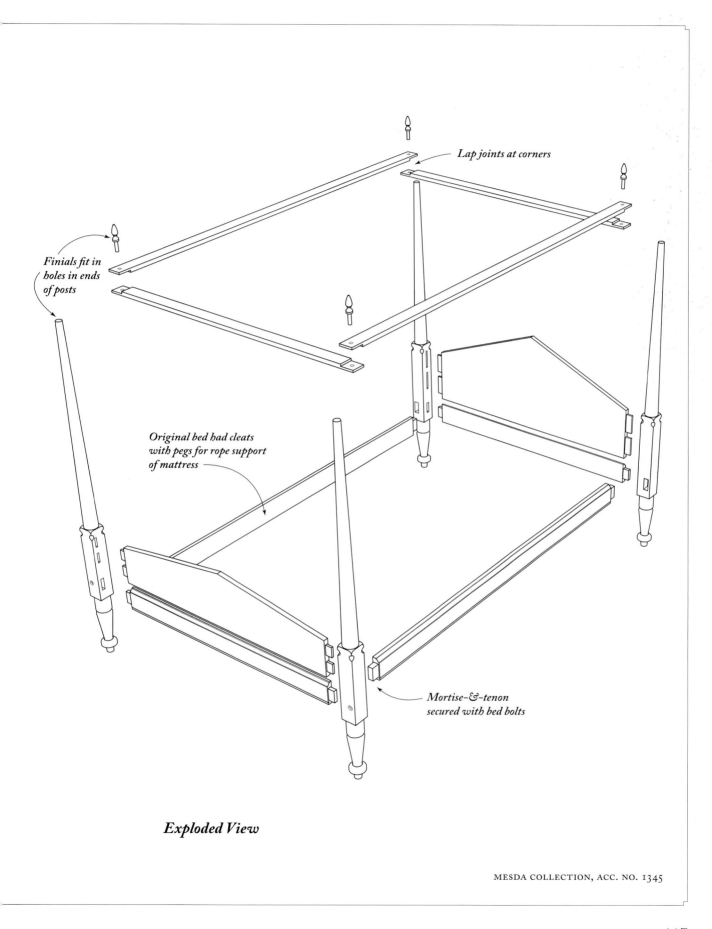

Lap joints at corners

Finials fit in
holes in ends
of posts

Original bed had cleats
with pegs for rope support
of mattress

Mortise-&-tenon
secured with bed bolts

**Exploded View**

MESDA COLLECTION, ACC. NO. 1345

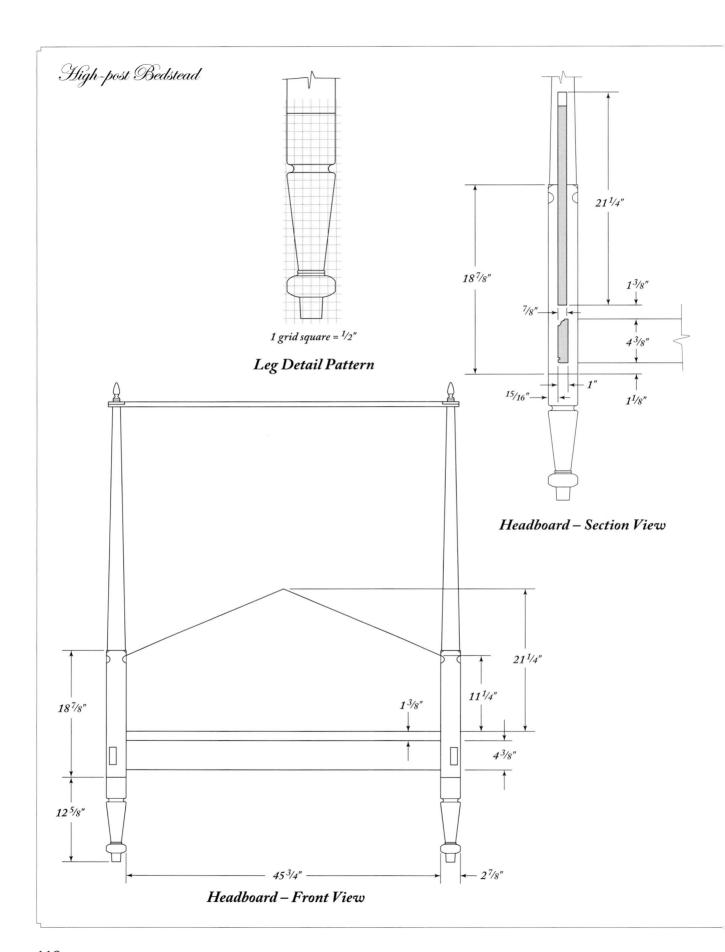

1 grid square = $^1/2$"

**Leg Detail Pattern**

21$^1/4$"

18$^7/8$"

1$^3/8$"

$^7/8$"

4$^3/8$"

1"

$^{15}/_{16}$"

1$^1/8$"

**Headboard – Section View**

21$^1/4$"

11$^1/4$"

18$^7/8$"

1$^3/8$"

4$^3/8$"

12$^5/8$"

45$^3/4$"

2$^7/8$"

**Headboard – Front View**

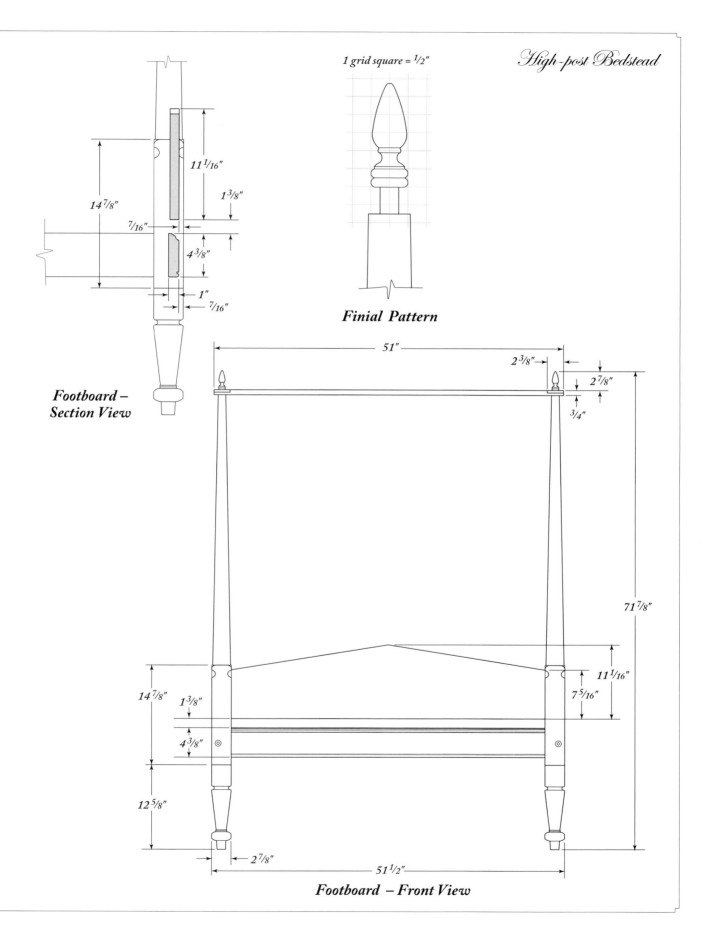

**1 grid square = 1/2"**

**Finial Pattern**

11 1/16"

1 3/8"

14 7/8"

7/16"

4 3/8"

1"

7/16"

**Footboard –
Section View**

51"

2 3/8"

2 7/8"

3/4"

71 7/8"

11 1/16"

7 5/16"

14 7/8"

1 3/8"

4 3/8"

12 5/8"

2 7/8"

51 1/2"

**Footboard – Front View**

# Blanket Chest with Drawers

*Built 1790–1800*
*in Salem, North Carolina*
*of walnut, poplar & yellow pine*

wo drawers below the main compartment of this blanket chest add additional storage, and make this chest tall and elegant in appearance. The bracket feet are simpler than on many pieces, with a single angled line intersecting a half circle instead of a more complex scrolled pattern. The connection of the feet to the bottom of the chest should be reinforced with glue blocks along the inner, top edge.

The case dovetails are through in the front and half-blind at the back. The exact till location and size are guesswork, so dimensions aren't shown. A typical till lid hinge dowel would be formed from the stock of the lid, rather than by inserting a separate dowel. The bottom of the interior is let in grooves on all four sides. The lower portion of the back may be treated as a separate piece and nailed in as shown, or the back could be made wider, with additional dovetails below the groove in the joint between the back and sides.

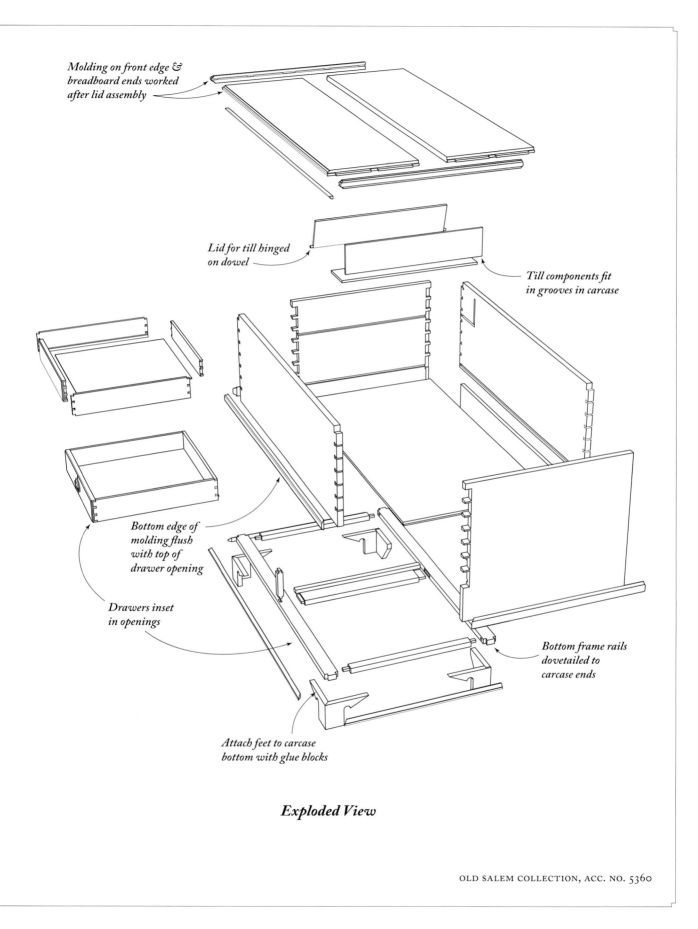

Molding on front edge &
breadboard ends worked
after lid assembly

Lid for till hinged
on dowel

Till components fit
in grooves in carcase

Bottom edge of
molding flush
with top of
drawer opening

Drawers inset
in openings

Bottom frame rails
dovetailed to
carcase ends

Attach feet to carcase
bottom with glue blocks

**Exploded View**

OLD SALEM COLLECTION, ACC. NO. 5360

# Blanket Chest with Drawers

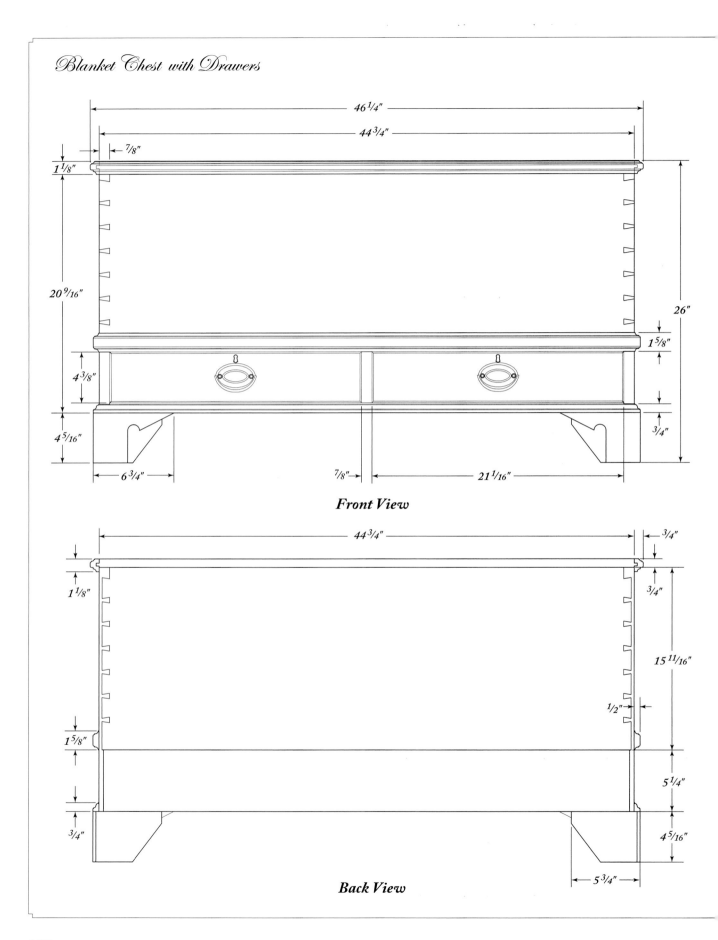

**Front View**

**Back View**

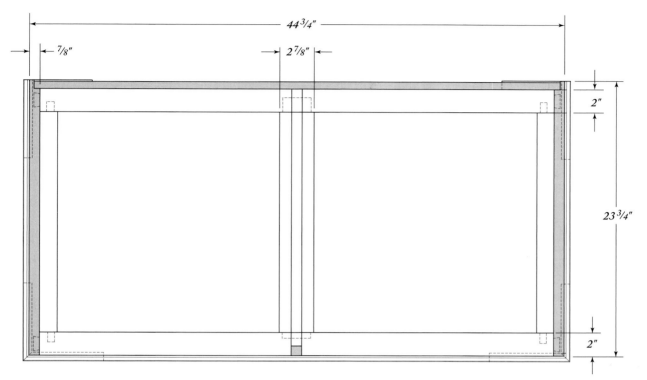

**Section Through Drawer Opening**

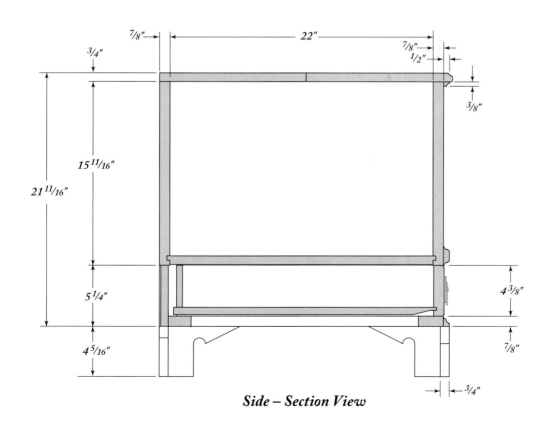

**Side – Section View**

# Low-post Bedstead

*Built 1800–1825*
*most likely in the Upper Valley of Virginia*
*of poplar & yellow pine, painted*

Southern furniture makers had a real knack for combining simple lines with curves in an attractive composition. As with the High-post Bedstead on page 116, this bed pre-dates standard sizes for mattresses, so the modern builder will need to adjust the lengths of all the rails between the posts to fit. The arrangement for supporting the mattress will also need to be updated. Secondary rails inside the outer rails will provide support, and bed bolts will allow the bed to be taken apart for moving.

Finding stock thick enough for the posts may also be a challenge for today's furniture maker. The posts can be laminated from thinner material. For the best appearance, choose straight-grained material from the same board for each post, and orient the glue lines so that they are in the least-visible position.

The ogee profiles on the top and bottom edges of the lower rails add a stylish detail to an otherwise-plain composition. The original bed was made of poplar and painted blue.

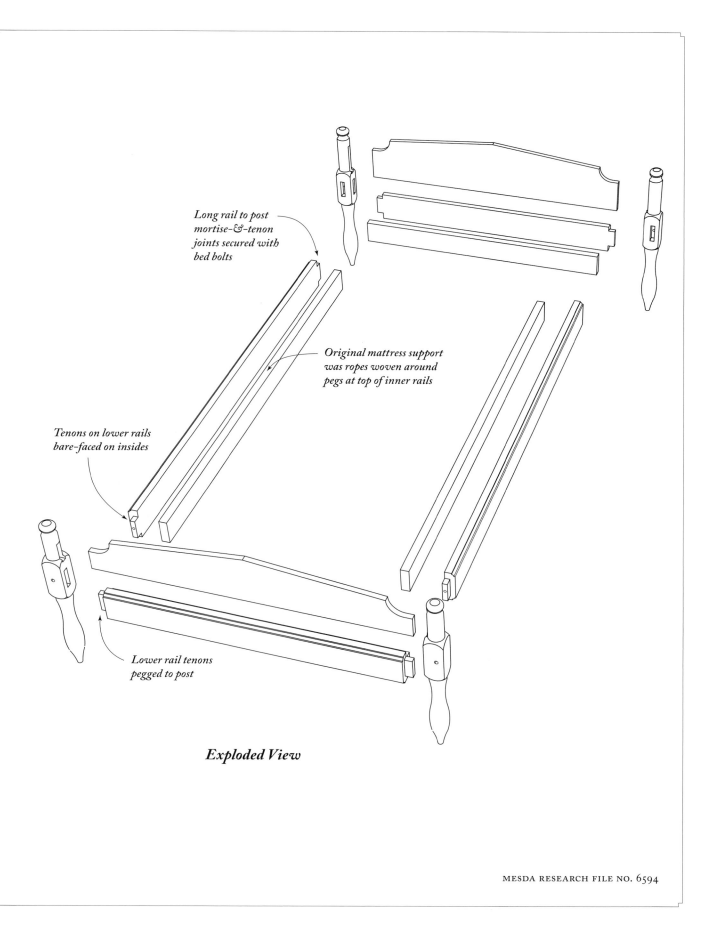

Long rail to post
mortise-&-tenon
joints secured with
bed bolts

Original mattress support
was ropes woven around
pegs at top of inner rails

Tenons on lower rails
bare-faced on insides

Lower rail tenons
pegged to post

**Exploded View**

MESDA RESEARCH FILE NO. 6594

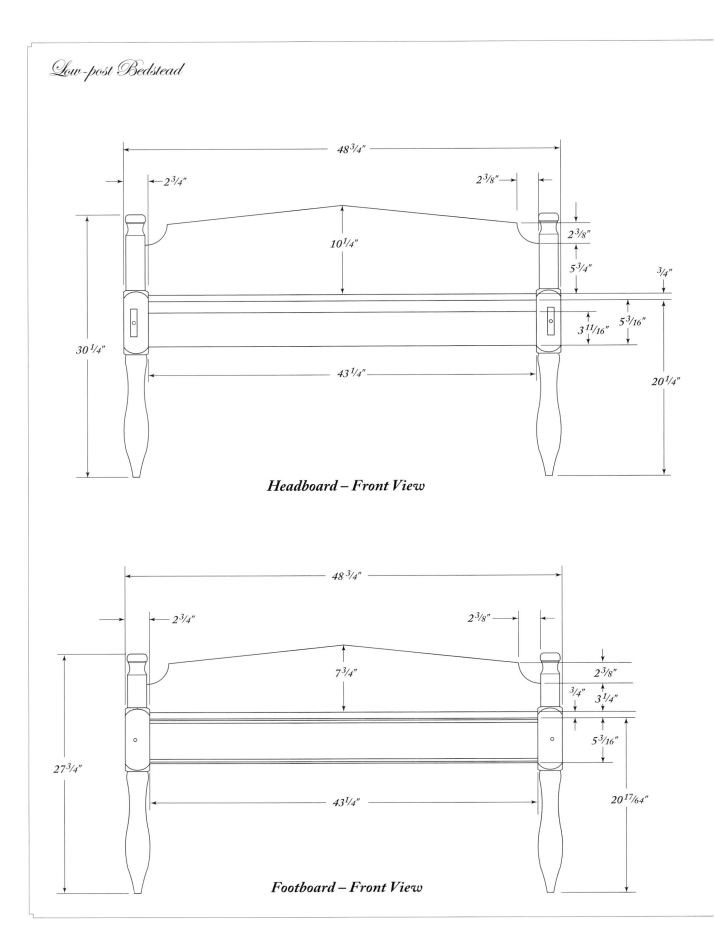

**Headboard – Front View**

**Footboard – Front View**

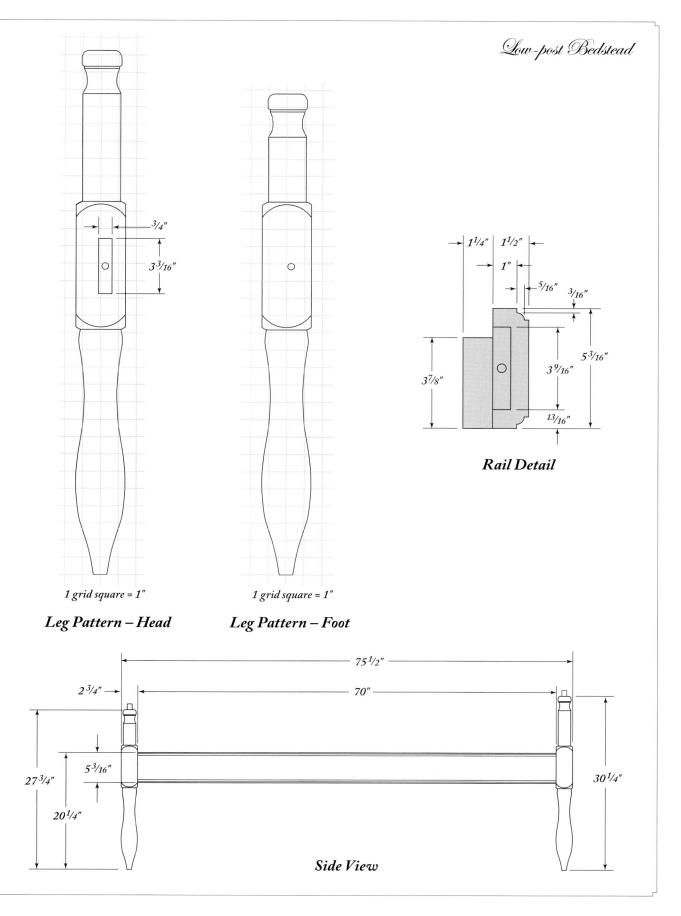

**Rail Detail**

1 grid square = 1"

**Leg Pattern – Head**

1 grid square = 1"

**Leg Pattern – Foot**

**Side View**

# Blanket Chest

*Built 1816
in Guilford County, North Carolina
of walnut & poplar*

Although this chest was not made in the Moravian community at Salem, the method of attaching cleats to the underside of the top is characteristic of many pieces from that North Carolina community. A sliding dovetail connects the cleat to the top, effectively holding the top from warping. This joint can be difficult to assemble, because the entire length of the cleat has to be inserted from one end.

The carcase is dovetailed front and back with half-blind joints, so that the joinery is not visible from the ends. The feet are somewhat unusual. Instead of being dovetailed or mitered on the front edge, the joint is a rabbet reinforced with wooden pegs. The connection between feet and chest is less than ideal, as the feet land outside the case thus making the molding a structural element. In the original, the back right foot and part of the front right foot have been replaced. In addition, some of the pointed ends of the scroll on the feet have broken.

Inside the box, there is a hidden drawer within the till, accessible by sliding the front of the till up. A hole in the bottom of the till provides a way to reach in from below to push the drawer out of its enclosure.

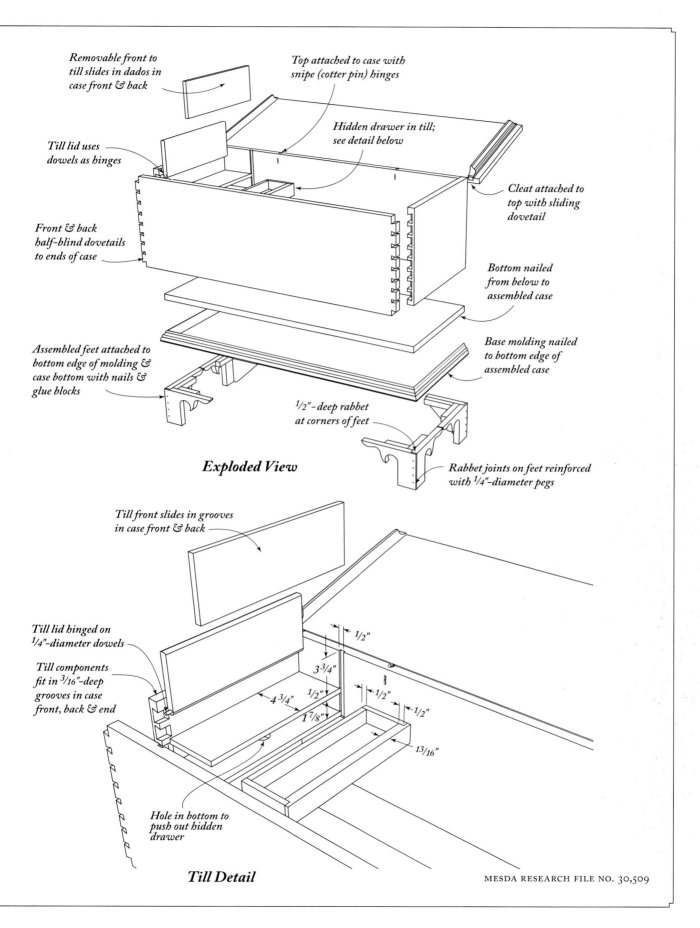

Removable front to
till slides in dados in
case front & back

Top attached to case with
snipe (cotter pin) hinges

Hidden drawer in till;
see detail below

Till lid uses
dowels as hinges

Cleat attached to
top with sliding
dovetail

Front & back
half-blind dovetails
to ends of case

Bottom nailed
from below to
assembled case

Assembled feet attached to
bottom edge of molding &
case bottom with nails &
glue blocks

Base molding nailed
to bottom edge of
assembled case

$1/2$"- deep rabbet
at corners of feet

**Exploded View**

Rabbet joints on feet reinforced
with $1/4$"-diameter pegs

Till front slides in grooves
in case front & back

Till lid hinged on
$1/4$"-diameter dowels

Till components
fit in $3/16$"-deep
grooves in case
front, back & end

$1/2$"

$3^3/4$"

$4^3/4$"    $1/2$"    $1/2$"    $1/2$"

$1^7/8$"

$13/16$"

Hole in bottom to
push out hidden
drawer

**Till Detail**

MESDA RESEARCH FILE NO. 30,509

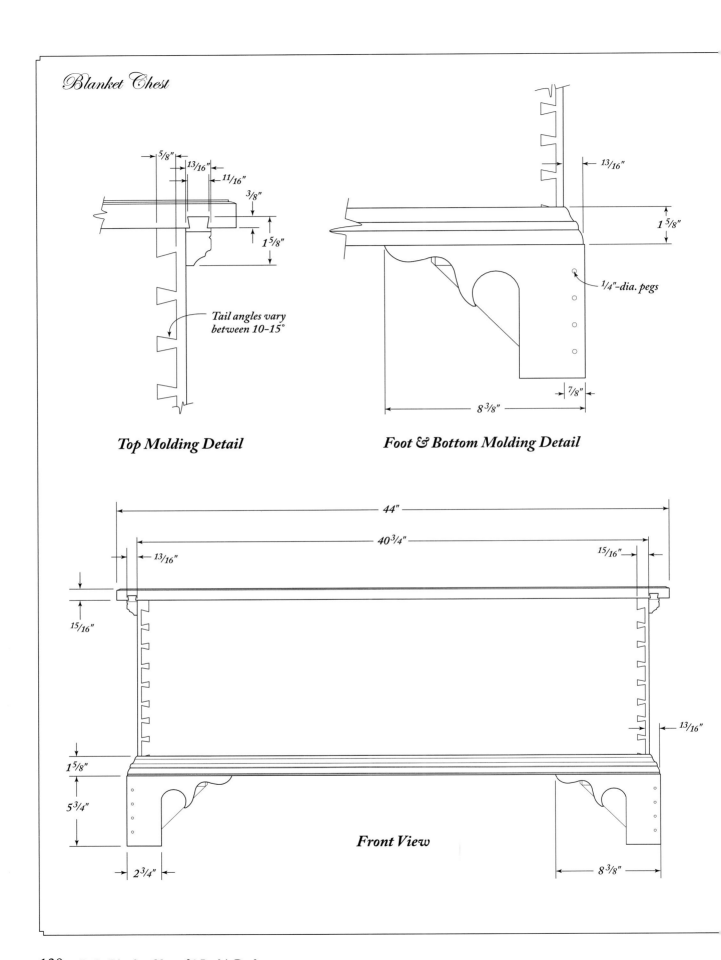

5/8"

13/16"

11/16"

3/8"

1 5/8"

Tail angles vary
between 10–15°

**Top Molding Detail**

13/16"

1 5/8"

1/4"-dia. pegs

7/8"

8 3/8"

**Foot & Bottom Molding Detail**

44"

40 3/4"

13/16"

15/16"

15/16"

13/16"

1 5/8"

5 3/4"

**Front View**

2 3/4"

8 3/8"

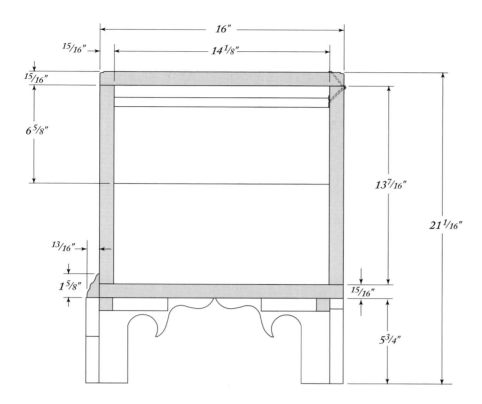

**Side – Section View**

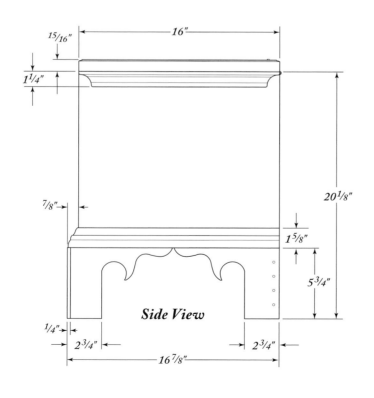

**Side View**

# Lady's Desk

*Built 1795–1805*
*in Wilmington, North Carolina*
*of mahogany, yellow pine & poplar*

This small desk was likely used in a bedroom, and while few people write letters with pen and paper today, we all need a place to organize the bills and keep the laptop computer. Measuring slightly less than 2' wide, this is a stylish and compact home office, and as a woodworking project, it offers the opportunity to practice many details with a minimal investment in material.

### Discrete Joinery

The hidden dovetail joints at the upper corners of the top section are a challenging detail, and a reminder that today's attitudes about joinery were not shared by our ancestors. Without a molding to cover the joints, this method provides strength and a neat appearance.

Other details, such as the cockbeading on the two large drawers, the graceful tapered legs and the use of mahogany as the primary wood, reflect the coastal origins of this desk. Cabinetmakers in port cities used methods that were closer to those used in England at the time, and they were directly competing with furniture made across the Atlantic or up the coast.

The inclusion of a pencil drawer between the two sliding supports for the drop front complicates the construction, but adds a useful feature. All of the drawers are joined with half-blind dovetails at the front, and through-dovetails at the back. In the large, lower drawers the bottoms are beveled on the front and sides to fit into a groove, with glue blocks between the bevels and the sides of the drawers. The bottoms of the smaller drawers in the top section are attached from below with cut nails, another difference in attitudes and construction methods between then and now.

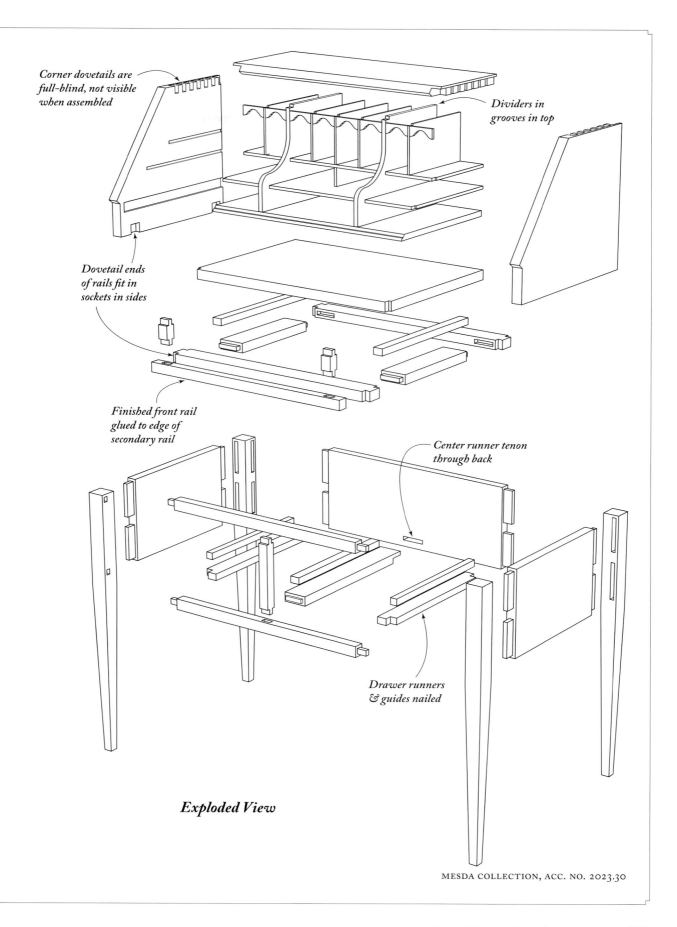

Corner dovetails are
full-blind, not visible
when assembled

Dividers in
grooves in top

Dovetail ends
of rails fit in
sockets in sides

Finished front rail
glued to edge of
secondary rail

Center runner tenon
through back

Drawer runners
& guides nailed

**Exploded View**

MESDA COLLECTION, ACC. NO. 2023.30

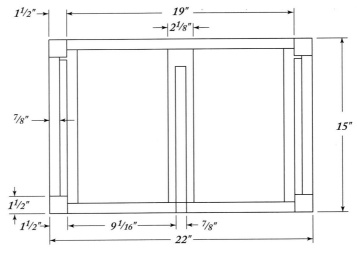

**Base – Top View**

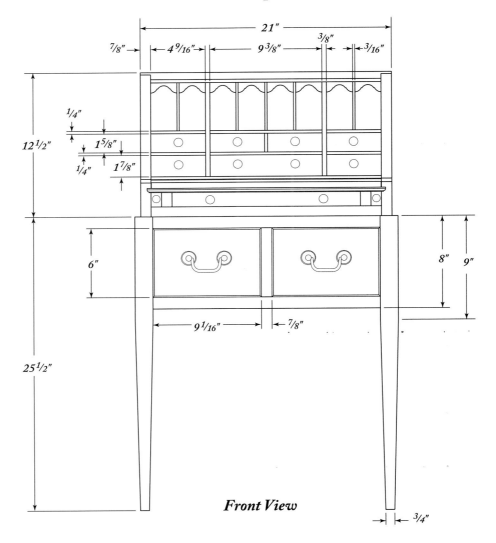

**Front View**

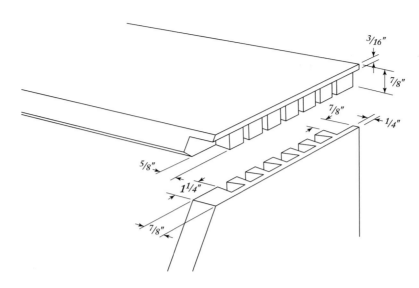

**Upper Case Dovetail Detail**

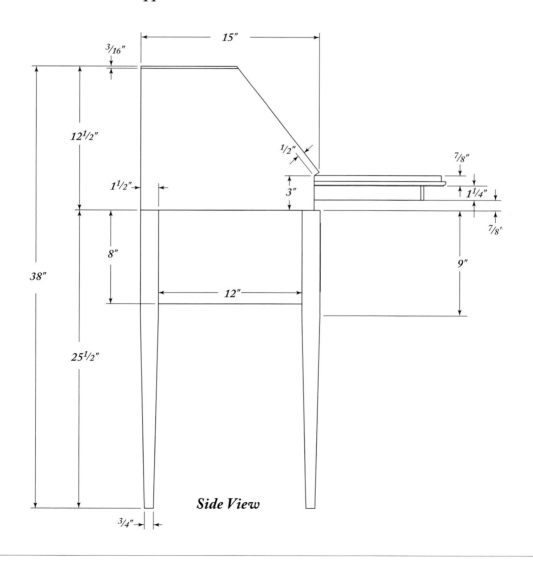

**Side View**

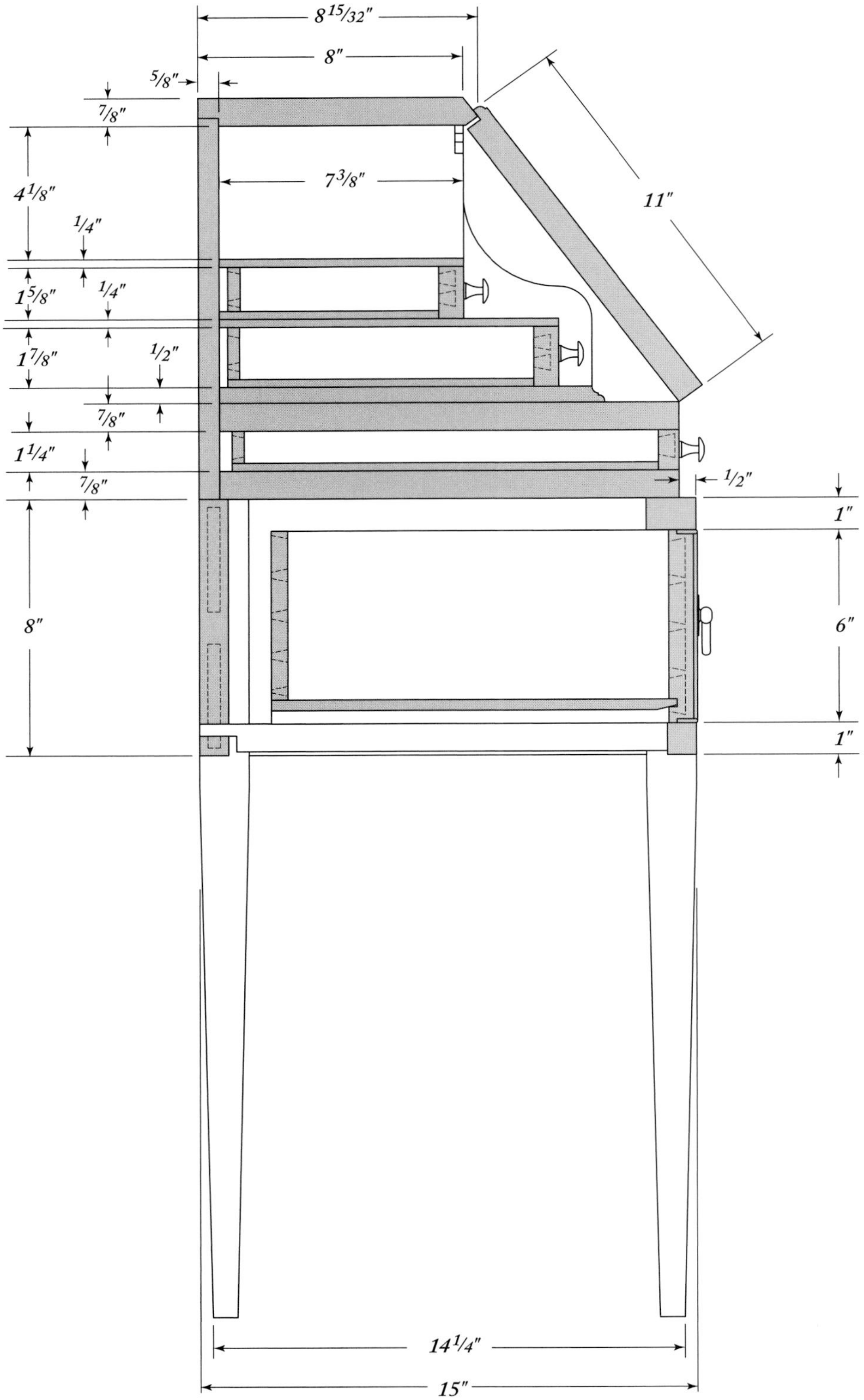

8 15/32"

8"

5/8"

7/8"

7 3/8"

4 1/8"

1/4"

1/4"

1 5/8"

1 7/8"

1/2"

11"

7/8"

1 1/4"

7/8"

1/2"

1"

8"

6"

1"

14 1/4"

15"

**Side – Section View**

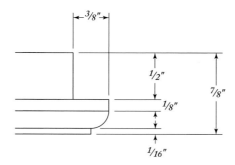

### Drop-front Molding Detail

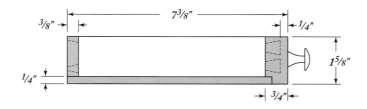

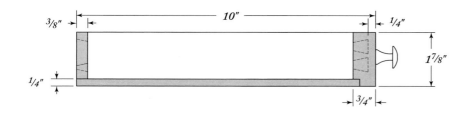

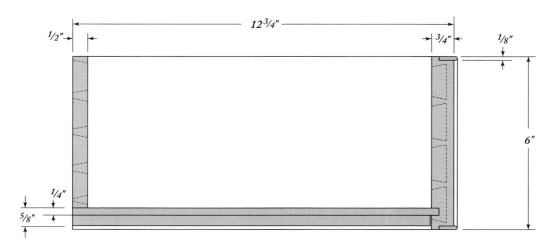

### Drawer Details

# Miscellaneous

# Cutlery Tray

⌒

*Built 1810–1820*
*possibly in North Carolina*
*of walnut, with light & dark wood inlay*
*& light wood stringing*

Museum notes suggest that this piece was made in North Carolina, but the style of the inlay is typical of many pieces made in Kentucky. Much of Kentucky was settled by North Carolinians moving north and west, and this may explain the similarities. Several small pieces of the light-colored stringing are now missing in the original piece.

The ends of the handle are in a V shape and slide into V-shaped grooves in the ends. In the period, this was a method for fitting thin pieces, used instead of a flat-bottomed dado. This shape is easier to fit precisely with a plane than an end-grain surface would be.

The dovetails in the original are slightly irregular, but the centerlines of the pins are perpendicular to the angled ends of the side pieces. The edges around the top of the open hopper and of the handle are gently rounded to make this small piece friendly to the hand as well as to the eye. The rounded edges of the bottom extend beyond the container and the bottom is attached with small cut nails.

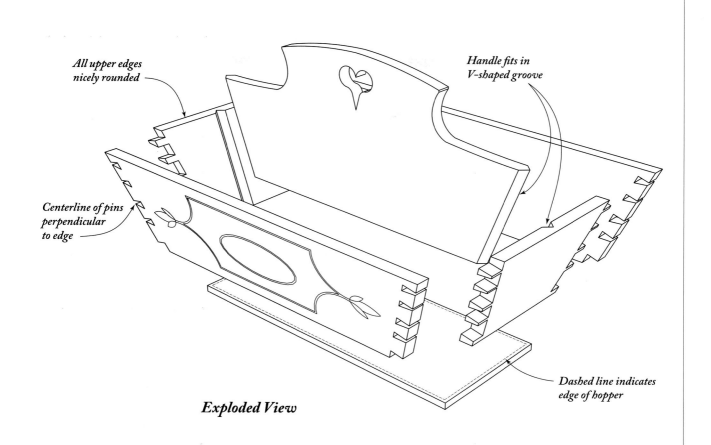

*All upper edges nicely rounded*

*Handle fits in V-shaped groove*

*Centerline of pins perpendicular to edge*

*Dashed line indicates edge of hopper*

**Exploded View**

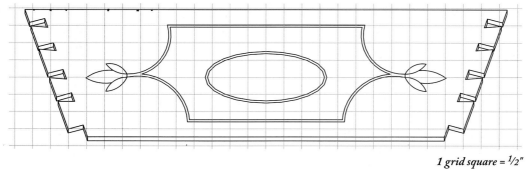

*1 grid square = ¹/₂″*

**Inlay Pattern**

MESDA COLLECTION, ACC. NO. 4850

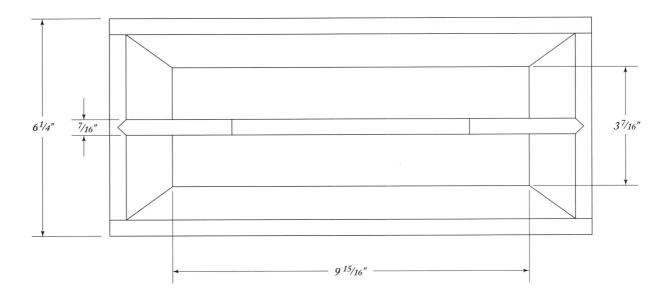

**Top View**

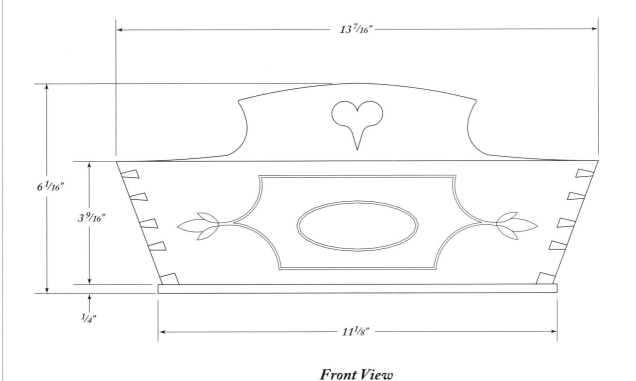

**Front View**

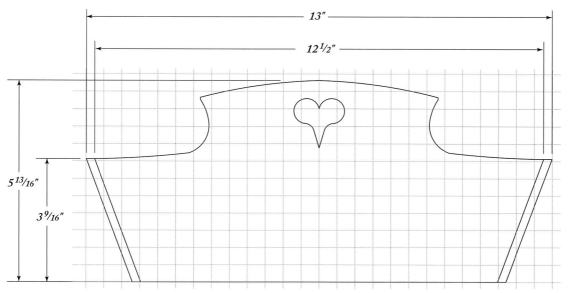

13"

12 1/2"

5 13/16"

3 9/16"

1 grid square = 1/2"

**Handle Pattern**

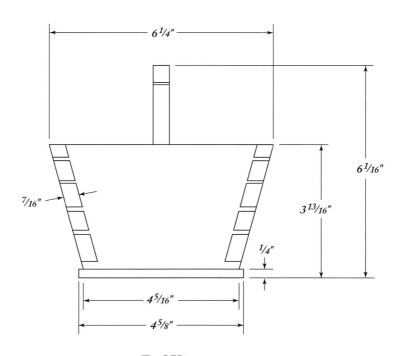

6 1/4"

6 1/16"

7/16"

3 13/16"

1/4"

4 5/16"

4 5/8"

**End View**

# Pinwheel Cabinet

*Built 1780–1790*
*most likely in the Catawba River Valley, North Carolina*
*of walnut, yellow pine & maple*

This diminutive cabinet contains big details, and many of the parts require thick stock. The arched top is sawn from a single piece of wood, as are the feet and lower molding. Behind the door, the drawer fronts are also thick, but relieved in the center to provide room for the brass knobs. At the top front of the case, the dovetail joint ends in a rabbeted miter to fit the arched rail above the door.

The overall form is similar to the hood of a tall case clock, and at the bottom of the case, the tails in the sides are reduced in height to allow the base molding to cover the joinery. The carved scrolls at each side add an architectural detail, both in themselves and in the short returns of the cornice molding. In contrast to the formality of the scrolls, the fylfot (pinwheel) and relatively wide stringing suggest a country rather than city origin.

The drawer bottoms are nailed to the sides and back of the drawer boxes, but there is a half-dovetailed rabbet in the lower edge of the drawer front where the front of the bottom attaches. Although this is similar in size and configuration to northern spice boxes, the museum notes state that this was used to store valuables other than spices.

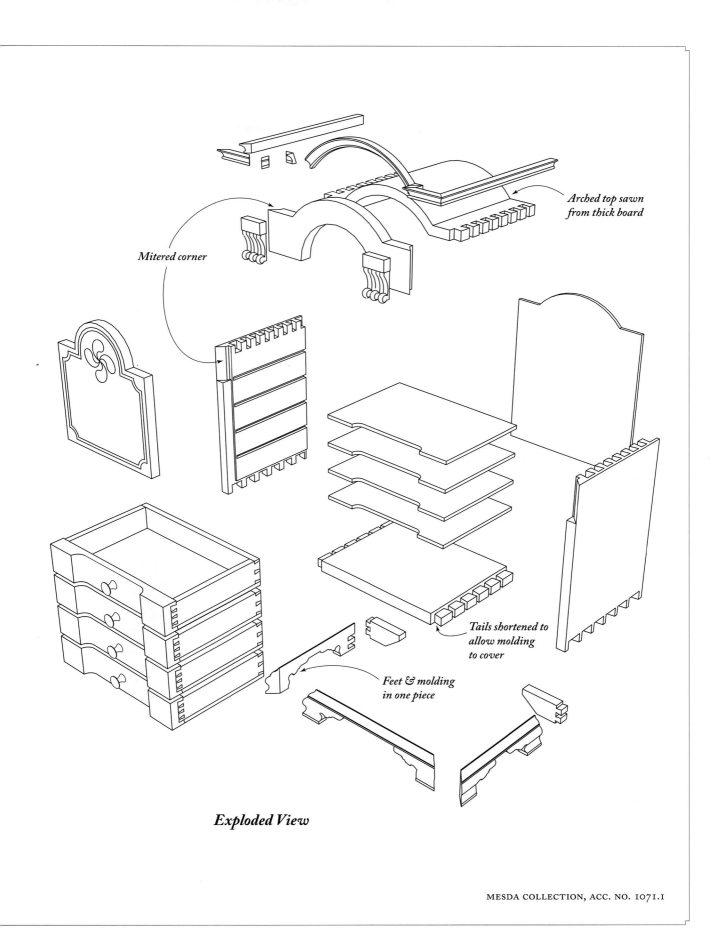

Arched top sawn
from thick board

Mitered corner

Tails shortened to
allow molding
to cover

Feet & molding
in one piece

**Exploded View**

MESDA COLLECTION, ACC. NO. 1071.1

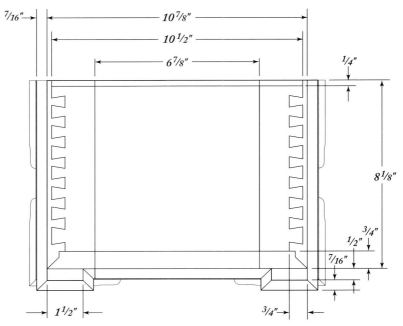

7/16"  10 7/8"  10 1/2"  6 7/8"  1/4"  8 1/8"  3/4"  1/2"  7/16"  1 1/2"  3/4"

**Top View**

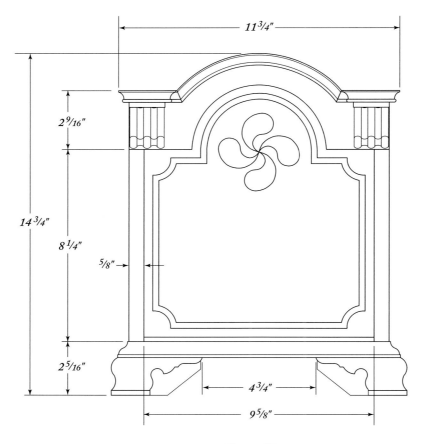

11 3/4"  2 9/16"  14 3/4"  8 1/4"  5/8"  2 5/16"  4 3/4"  9 5/8"

**Front View**

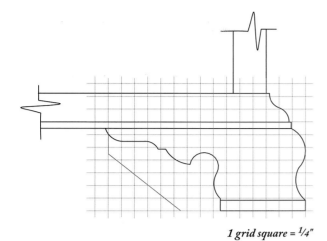

1 grid square = ¹/₄"

**Foot Pattern**

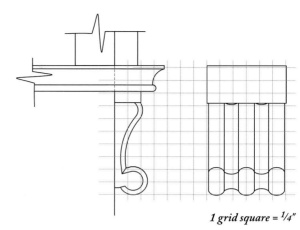

1 grid square = ¹/₄"

**Corbel Detail**

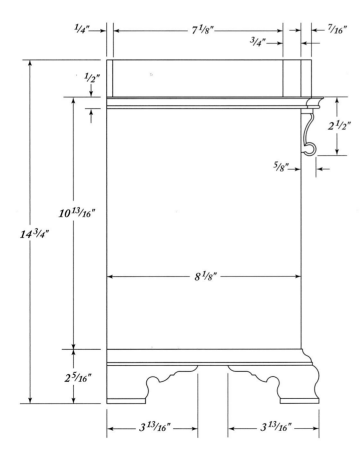

¹/₄"    7¹/₈"    ⁷/₁₆"

³/₄"

¹/₂"

2¹/₂"

5/8"

10¹³/₁₆"

14³/₄"

8¹/₈"

2⁵/₁₆"

3¹³/₁₆"    3¹³/₁₆"

**Side View**

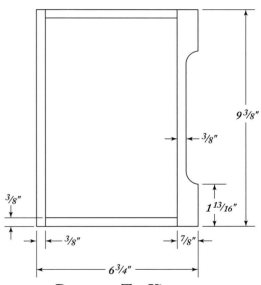

9³/₈"

3/8"

1¹³/₁₆"

3/8"

3/8"    7/8"

6³/₄"

**Drawer – Top View**

¹/₂"

1¹/₂"

1¹³/₁₆"

¹/₄"

7/8"

**Drawer – Side View**

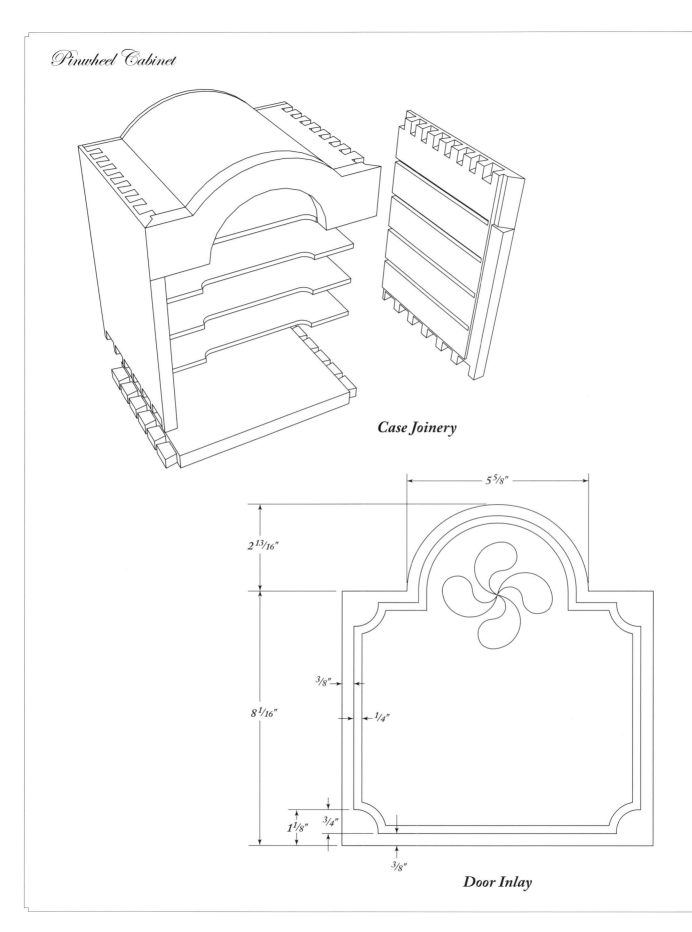

*Pinwheel Cabinet*

**Case Joinery**

5 ⅝"

2 ¹³⁄₁₆"

8 ¹⁄₁₆"

⅜"

¼"

1 ⅛"   ¾"

⅜"

**Door Inlay**

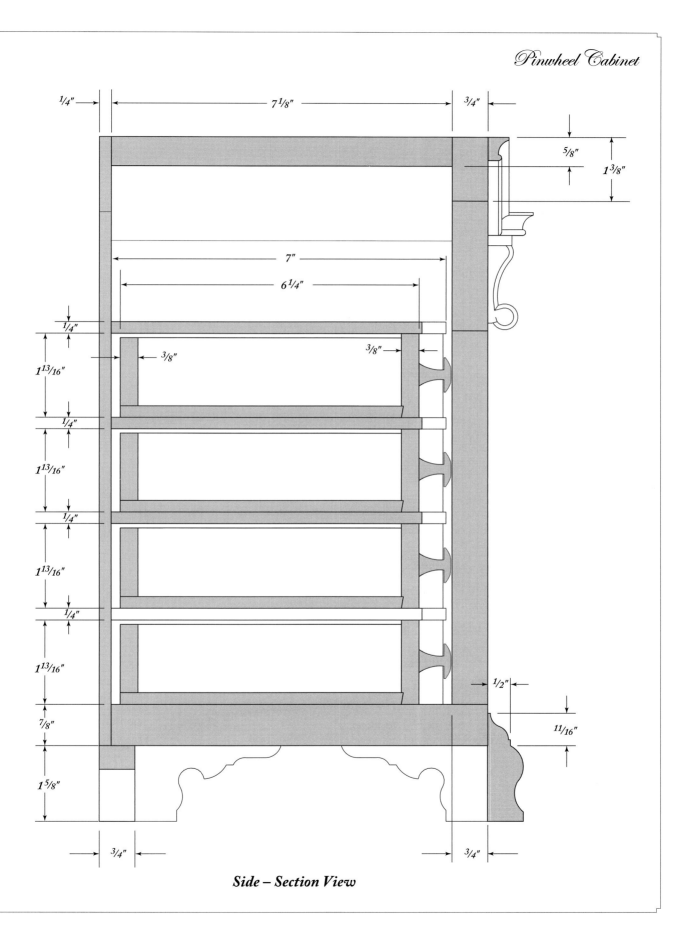

**Side – Section View**

# Inlaid Box

*Built circa 1763*
*most likely in western Maryland*
*of walnut with light wood inlay*

This small valuables box is a study in contrasts. The joinery and molding of the breadboard ends on the top is intricate, yet the bottom of the box is simply nailed on. The design of the inlay is complex, but the execution, especially at the corners of the banding, is somewhat primitive. Overall, it's a box with a lot of character; the maker obviously spent a lot of time in constructing this special piece. The fact that it survived for almost 250 years is a testament to the care of the maker and to subsequent owners.

The tulip inlays on the top and front are a series of connected arcs, apparently laid out with a compass. Our drawing of the top shows where the pieces of the curved branches were joined end to end, allowing the grain to better follow the curves. These joints were probably less visible when the box was made. The inlay also would have been flush to the surface. Wood movement has left the inlay slightly proud, but it is still intact and in excellent condition.

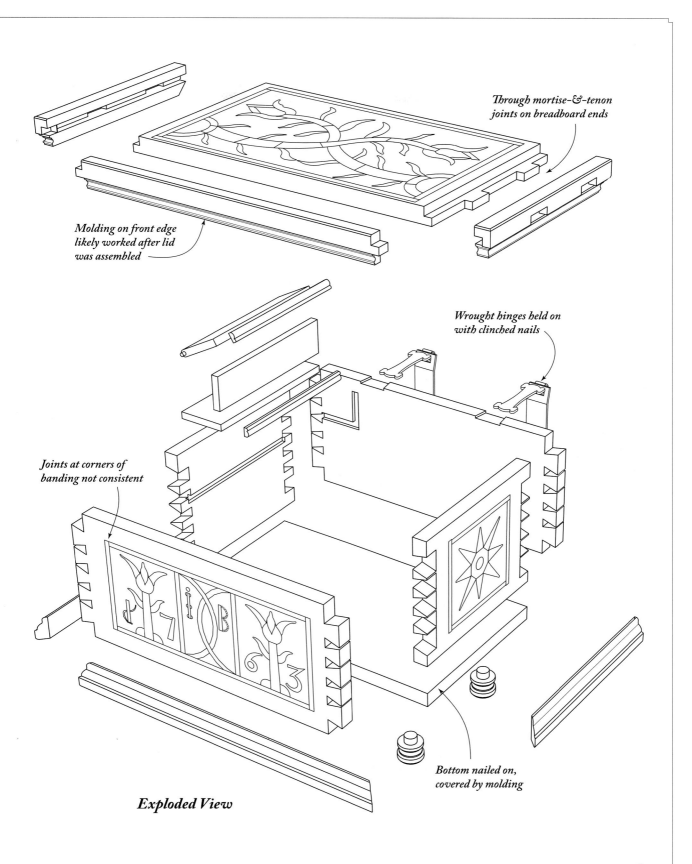

Through mortise-&-tenon
joints on breadboard ends

Molding on front edge
likely worked after lid
was assembled

Wrought hinges held on
with clinched nails

Joints at corners of
banding not consistent

Bottom nailed on,
covered by molding

**Exploded View**

MESDA COLLECTION, ACC. NO. 4987

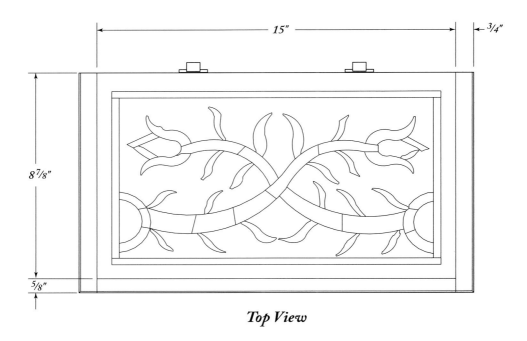

**Top View**

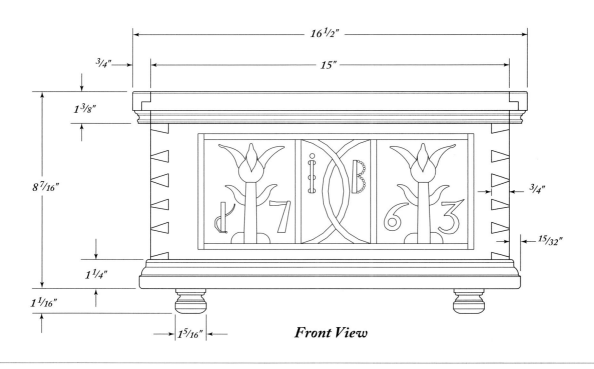

**Front View**

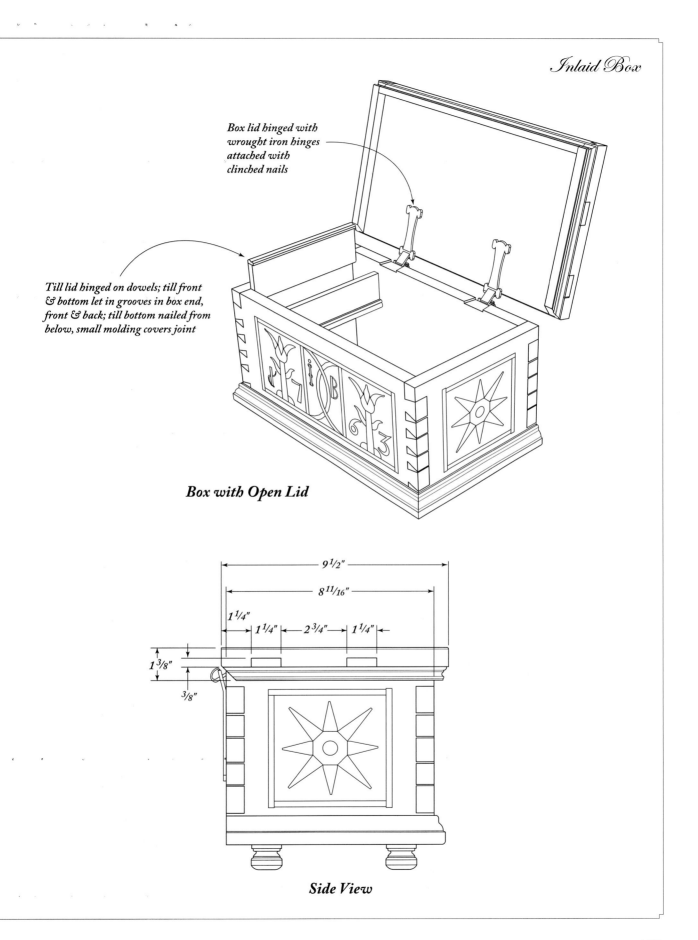

Box lid hinged with
wrought iron hinges
attached with
clinched nails

Till lid hinged on dowels; till front
& bottom let in grooves in box end,
front & back; till bottom nailed from
below, small molding covers joint

**Box with Open Lid**

9½"

8¹¹⁄₁₆"

1¼"

1¼"  2¾"  1¼"

1³⁄₈"

³⁄₈"

**Side View**

# Tall Case Clock

*Built circa 1820
in Salem, North Carolina
of walnut*

This tall clock owes its handsome appearance to great proportions, not to decoration. This no-frills approach lends an air of quiet dignity and authority. The overall composition makes it difficult to judge the size of this piece when it is seen out of context. It would be attractive at any height, but at just more than 7'-6" tall, it is a monumental piece.

Simple moldings set off the transitions between the three sections of the case, and simple bun feet raise it slightly off the floor. The Moravians in Salem did not have strict religious standards as some groups did, but their furniture tends toward the simple and practical form seen here. The moldings are ample in cross section, but simple in profile; there are soft ogees at the top and bottom, and coves combined with fillets in between.

The simple appearance doesn't mean a lack of detail or crude construction. The outer corners of the lower case are mitered, allowing the grain to flow uninterrupted from the front to the sides. The tall door in the midsection is a single panel, with mitered rails let in at the top and bottom, which is not an easy task in any time period.

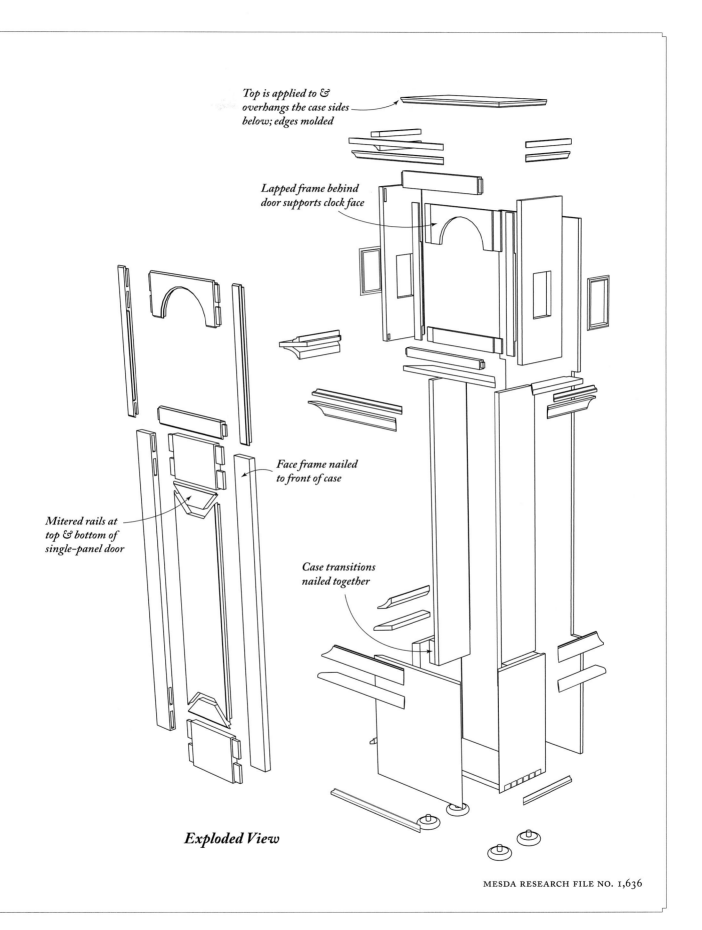

Top is applied to &
overhangs the case sides
below; edges molded

Lapped frame behind
door supports clock face

Face frame nailed
to front of case

Mitered rails at
top & bottom of
single-panel door

Case transitions
nailed together

**Exploded View**

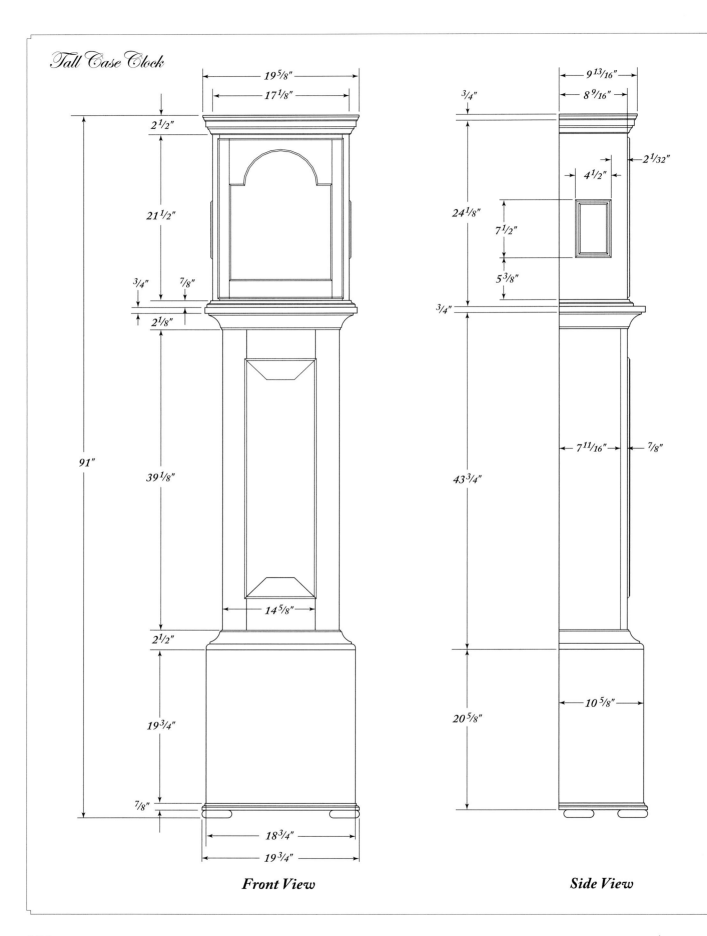

Tall Case Clock

**Front View**

**Side View**

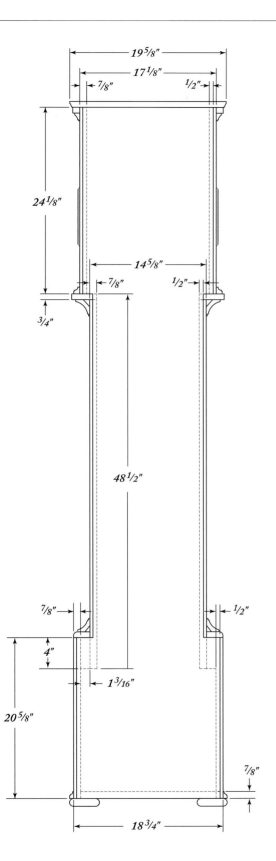

**Back View**

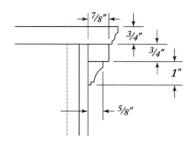

**Crown Molding**

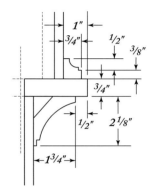

**Upper Transition Molding**

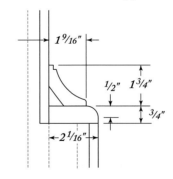

**Lower Transition Molding**

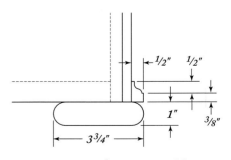

**Foot Detail & Base Molding**

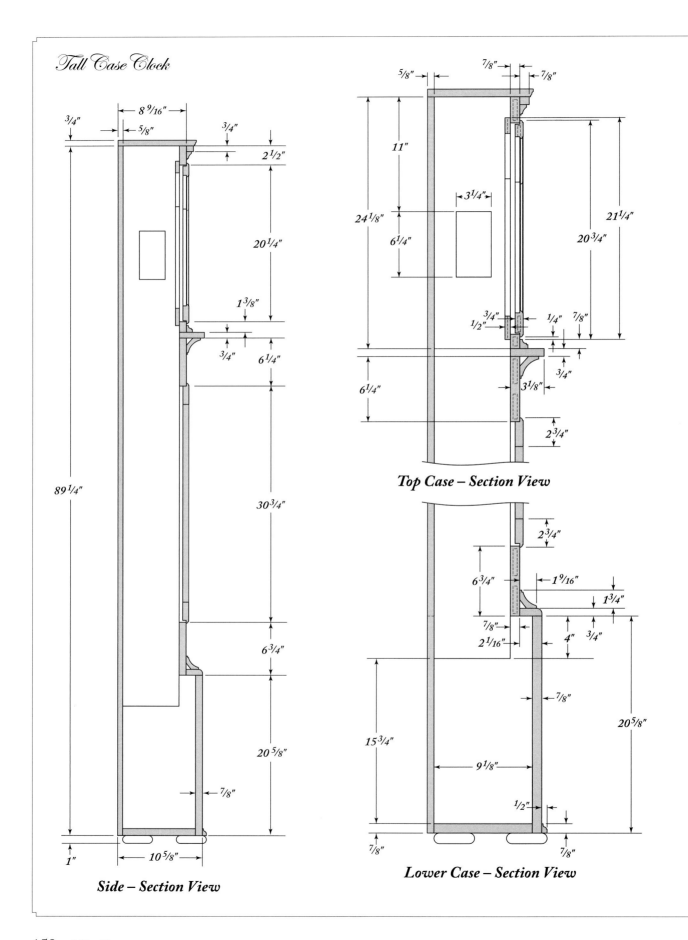

*Tall Case Clock*

8 9/16"

3/4"
5/8"
3/4"
2 1/2"

20 1/4"

1 3/8"
3/4"
6 1/4"

89 1/4"

30 3/4"

6 3/4"

20 5/8"

7/8"

1"
10 5/8"

**Side – Section View**

5/8"
7/8"
7/8"

11"

24 1/8"

3 1/4"

6 1/4"

21 1/4"

20 3/4"

3/4"
1/2"
1/4"
7/8"

6 1/4"

3/4"
3 1/8"

2 3/4"

**Top Case – Section View**

2 3/4"

6 3/4"
1 9/16"

1 3/4"

7/8"
2 1/16"
4"
3/4"

7/8"

20 5/8"

15 3/4"
9 1/8"

1/2"

7/8"
7/8"

**Lower Case – Section View**

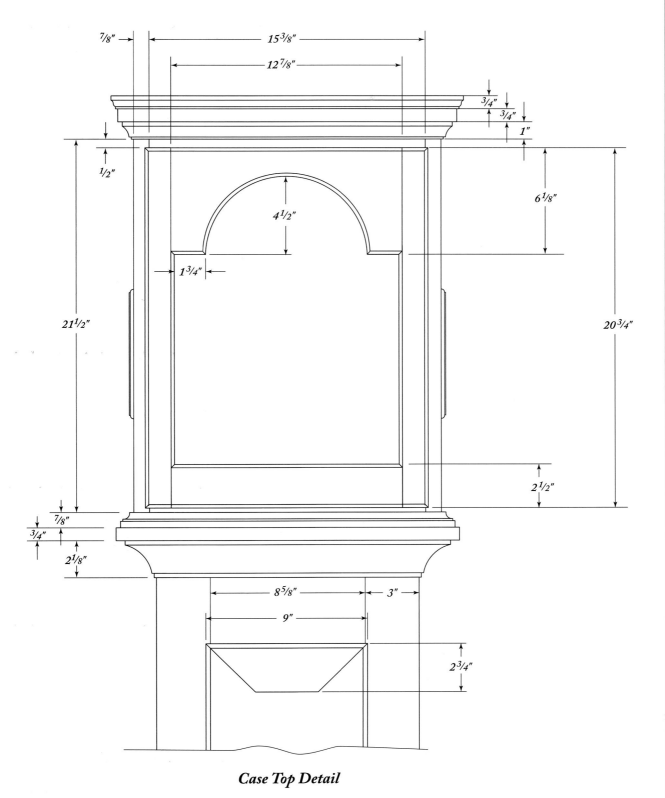

**Case Top Detail**

# Explore Southern Furniture with SketchUp

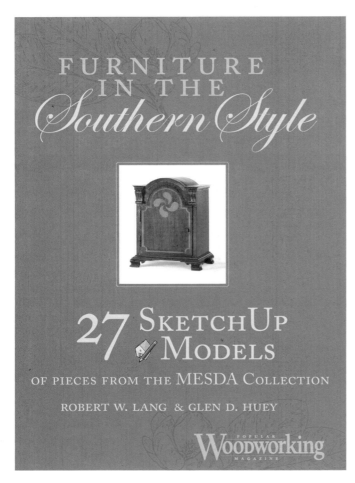

US $19.99 ▪ CAN $20.99 ▪ V0709

**Order your copy of "Furniture in the Southern Style: 27 SketchUp Models of Pieces from the MESDA Collection" at ShopWoodworking.com/mesda**

- Closely examine every part & every joint on your computer
- Develop & print detailed drawings & cutlists
- Explore construction details

On this companion CD to "Furniture in the Southern Style," you'll find the 27 detailed 3D Google SketchUp models the authors developed to create the book's print illustrations.

Install the free Google SketchUp software on your computer and you'll be able to closely examine, disassemble and reassemble, and modify the furniture pieces – or use the models as starting points for your own design. It's as close as you can come to physically taking apart examples of priceless antiques for study!

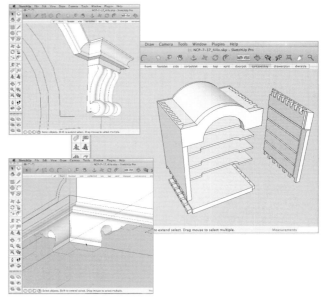

---

Other great **Popular Woodworking** products are available at your local bookstore, woodworking store or online supplier and from ShopWoodworking.com.

---

Visit **popularwoodworking.com** to see more woodworking information by the experts, learn about our digital subscription and sign up to receive our weekly newsletter at popularwoodworking.com/newsletters/

---

FOLLOW
POPULAR
WOODWORKING